KT-178-658

THE KNITTER'S BIBLE knitted accessories

BOURNEMOUTH LIBRARIES

620064392 W

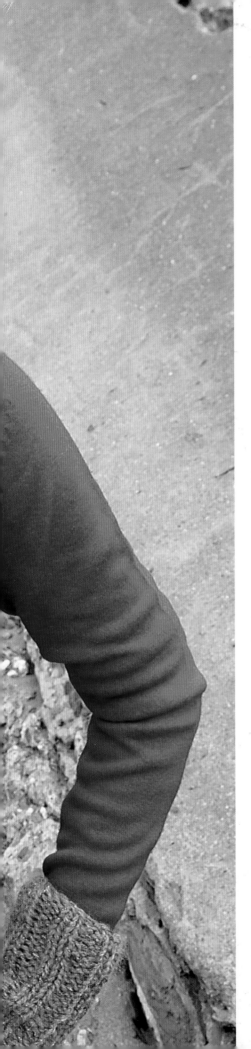

THE KNITTER'S BIBLE

knitted accessories

CLAIRE CROMPTON

BOURNEMOUTH

3 0 MAR 2007

LIBRARIES

D&C

David and Charles

A DAVID & CHARLES BOOK

Copyright © David & Charles Limited 2006

David & Charles is an F+W Publications Inc. company
4700 East Galbraith Road
Cincinnati, OH 45236

First published in the UK in 2006

Text and project designs © Claire Crompton 2006

Claire Crompton has asserted her right to be identified as author
of this work in accordance with the Copyright, Designs and Patents Act, 1988.

All rights reserved. No part of this publication may be reproduced,
stored in a retrieval system, or transmitted, in any form or by any means,
electronic or mechanical, by photocopying, recording or otherwise,
without prior permission in writing from the publisher.

The designs in this book are copyright and must not be made for resale.

A catalogue record for this book is available from the British Library.

ISBN-13: 978-0-7153-2327-4 wiro-bound
ISBN-10: 0-7153-2327-X wiro-bound

ISBN-13: 978-0-7153-2600-8 paperback
ISBN-10: 0-7153-2600-7 paperback

Printed in China by RR Donnelley
for David & Charles
Brunel House   Newton Abbot   Devon

Executive Editor Cheryl Brown
Editor Jennifer Proverbs
Head of Design Prudence Rogers
Production Controller Ros Napper
Project Editor Nicola Hodgson
Photographer Lorna Yabsley

Visit our website at www.davidandcharles.co.uk

David & Charles books are available from all good bookshops; alternatively
you can contact our Orderline on 0870 9908222 or write to us at FREEPOST EX2 110,
D&C Direct, Newton Abbot, TQ12 4ZZ (no stamp required UK only); US customers call
800-289-0963 and Canadian customers call 800-840-5220.

*The author and publisher have made every effort to ensure that all the instructions in the book
are accurate and safe, and therefore cannot accept liability for any resulting injury, damage or
loss to persons or property, however it may arise.*

*Names of manufacturers, paper ranges and other products are provided for the information of
readers, with no intention to infringe copyright or trademarks.*

contents

accessorize yourself!

Every stylish woman knows that accessories are the best way to turn an outfit from mundane to magnificent. This book of knitted accessories takes you through a range of fun and exciting projects, ranging from quick-to-knit scarves, chic but simple hats and funky mittens, to sophisticated gloves, shawls and ponchos that take a little more time and effort. Think of these projects as starting points for your own inspiration.

Throughout, I have concentrated on the yarns, using different textures together or mixing several yarns together to create a unique yarn, and suggested ways in which you can develop an idea further. Don't just stick to what I have done; experiment with daring colour combos, try unexpected textures together, or see how different stitches can look when worked in different weights of yarn. Create something unique of your own.

Natural fibres are always great to work with and there are so many exciting synthetic yarns to explore, too. The three yarn sections – fibres (page 9), weight (page 10) and texture (pages 12–13) – will help you identify yarns and enable you to substitute yarns confidently.

I have emphasized the need to measure your gauge (what knitters in the UK call tension) accurately. This section (page 15) deals with the importance of gauge and how to achieve it, with tips on how to measure gauge over heavily textured yarns. In each project I discuss the gauge that I achieved; use this information to experiment and create your own unique knitted fabrics.

All the projects in this book are for people with a basic knowledge of knitting. Some projects, such as the garter-stitch scarves and wrap (see pages 20–27), the Heads Up Hat (pages 28–31) and the easy mittens (pages 32–43) are designed to encourage beginners to try knitting accessories. But there is plenty here to inspire experienced knitters, too; for each project I have given ideas for using different yarns and colours. The 'Yarn Focus' feature is an explanation of why I chose a particular yarn for that project, while 'Design Secrets Unravelled…' suggests alternative yarns and colours to give the projects a different twist. I have knitted up several swatches in different yarns to illustrate this idea. I hope that you will be encouraged to choose yarns or colours that you wouldn't ordinarily use and try out textures that you have previously shied away from. Many of the projects are written in multiple sizes so you will achieve a good fit, especially on the gloves and hats.

All the techniques that are used to make the projects in this book are explained in detail in the resource section (pages 102–124), with clear diagrams and reference to the projects. If you require a more comprehensive guide to knitting techniques and instructions, my previous book, *The Knitter's Bible*, contains everything you need to know. If you want to recreate the projects exactly, there is a list of the yarns that I used (pages 125–126) and a comprehensive list of suppliers who stock those yarns (page 127).

So grab your needles, choose your yarn and start accessorizing!

in the beginning…

fibres

One of the joys of being a knitter is being able to explore the fabulous range of yarns that is available today. This is especially true of knitting accessories; you need a relatively small amount of yarn to make a hat, a pair of gloves, or a knitted corsage, so you can splash out and experiment with some of the more luxurious yarns. Or you can keep to tried-and-tested old favourites such as cotton and wool. The guide to fibres below will help you think about the textures, finish and weight of the various yarns around.

NATURAL FIBRES

Natural fibres come from either animal or plant sources. They can be more expensive than synthetic fibres, but you generally pay for quality. For everyday items that will get a lot of wear, a blend of natural fibres with more robust synthetic fibres is often a good option. The synthetic fibres often mean that your garment will be machine-washable rather than handwash only.

Alpaca is spun from the coat of the alpaca, a close relation of the llama. It is a wonderfully soft and lustrous yarn, which has many of the qualities of cashmere but comes at a more affordable price.

Angora hair comes from the Angora rabbit. A yarn with a high content of angora is very fluffy and sheds fibres. It is usually blended with another fibre to give it stability; it gives the yarn softness.

Cashmere is spun from the hair of the Cashmere goat. Pure cashmere yarn is very expensive and best kept for really exceptional garments. When it is blended with another fibre, it becomes much more affordable. I have used a cashmere/wool mix yarn for the Cashmere Chic Set (pages 78–83) because it is so luxurious.

Cotton comes from the ball of the cotton plant. It is a heavy fibre and is often blended with other fibres, such as silk or wool, to lighten it. It has no elasticity and so items knitted from it can tend to become baggy with wear. However, it is a great hot-weather fibre, often used in summer garments. Cotton can be mercerized; this is a process to give it lustre and allow it take brighter dyes. Matte cotton tends to be more loosely spun.

Linen comes from the stem of the flax plant, and is often blended with cotton to soften it. On its own, linen drapes better than cotton so makes elegant summer garments and lightweight scarves. It is available in fashion colours as well as more traditional natural shades.

Mohair is spun from the coat of the Angora goat. The softer kid mohair is the first or second shearing of a kid goat and is finer than the mohair from the adult goat. It is usually blended with another fibre to give it strength. I have used it for the Heads Up Hat (pages 28–31) and Bramble Stitch Lacy Shawl (pages 62–65), where it is blended with nylon and wool, and in a yarn mix for the Good Things Come in Threes set (pages 48–53), where it is blended with a luxurious silk. It also appears in the Making Waves Scarf (pages 54–57), where it is part of a fantastic ribbon yarn. I use mohair because it is light, and it adds texture and a haze of colour into a yarn mix.

Silk is a continuous filament secreted by the silkworm larva, which it spins around itself to form a cocoon. The cocoon is unwound and many of the fibres are spun together to form a yarn. Silk has a lovely lustre; it is also soft and has a dry feel. I have used it in the Winter Warmer Scarf (page 77), where it is blended with cotton.

Wool is spun from the fleece of a sheep; different breeds of sheep produce different qualities of yarn. Merino wool is very soft; Shetland is more hardwearing; Wensleydale is very lustrous; and Jacob wool is spun in fantastic natural colours. Wool has excellent insulating qualities; it is warm in winter and cool in summer. Many of the projects in this book use wool, and I would always recommend it as a great yarn for a beginner to use. It knits up beautifully and can be pulled back and recycled without loss of quality.

BLENDED AND SYNTHETIC FIBRES

Blends of natural and synthetic fibres combine the natural yarn's qualities with the hardwearing and stable features of the synthetic yarn. Some of the synthetic fibres used in the projects are acrylic, metallic, microfibre, nylon, polyamide fibre, polyester and viscose. Synthetic fibres are spun into wonderful fancy yarns, such as eyelash, ribbon and faux fur. They also take dyes well.

weight

The weight of a yarn is one of the factors that you can experiment with when you are exploring your own knitting creativity. A knitted stitch can look very different when worked in a chunky, heavy yarn than when it is knitted in a light and airy one. Just compare the Classic Cabled Poncho and the Cobweb Cabled Wrap (pages 96–101). One looks as deliciously thick and warm as a blanket; the other is a beautifully soft and delicate fabric – and yet the same stitch was used for both garments.

PLY OR THICKNESS

A ply is a single twisted strand. As a general rule, the more plies that are twisted together, the thicker the yarn. However, just to confuse things, plies from different yarn manufacturers can be different thicknesses themselves. A tightly spun ply will be thinner than a loosely spun one. For example, a 2ply Shetland wool yarn knits up to fine-weight (4ply) gauge, whereas a thick Lopi yarn (a type of wool traditionally sourced from Iceland) is a single ply.

To avoid this confusion, I have adopted a standard developed by the Craft Yarn Council of America, which divides yarns into weights rather than number of plies. Throughout this book, I have given a generic description of each yarn used, specifying the weight and type of yarn that I have used for each project. This means that you can use any yarn that is the same weight to knit your project. (If you want to use exactly the same yarns featured in the book, see pages 125–126 for details.)

Yarn manufacturers in the US and in the UK sometimes use different names to identify the same weight of yarn. Where they differ, I have included both in the following table. Throughout this book, I give the US yarn weight first, with the UK equivalent following in brackets.

STANDARD YARN WEIGHTS

weight	gauge*	needle size**	yarn type***
super-fine	27–32 sts	1 to 3 (2.25–3.25mm)	sock, fingering (2ply, 3ply)
fine	23–26 sts	3 to 5 (3.25–3.75mm)	sport, baby (4ply)
light	21–24 sts	5 to 7 (3.75–4.5mm)	light worsted, DK (DK)
medium	16–20 sts	7 to 9 (4.5–5.5mm)	worsted, afghan (aran)
bulky	12–15 sts	9 to 11 (5.5–8mm)	chunky
super-bulky	6–11 sts	11 (8mm) and above	super-chunky

Notes:
* Gauge (tension) is measured over 4in/10cm in stockinette (stocking) stitch
** US needle sizes are given first, with UK equivalents in brackets
*** Alternative US yarn type names are given first, with UK equivalents in brackets

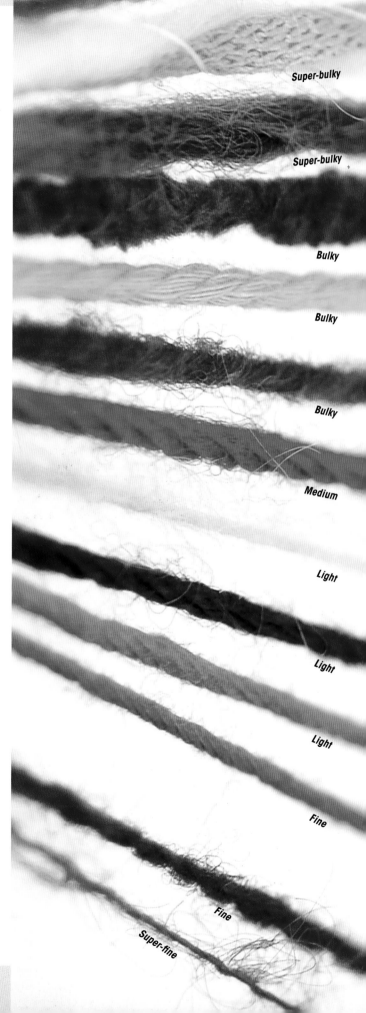

Super-bulky

Super-bulky

Bulky

Bulky

Bulky

Medium

Light

Light

Light

Fine

Fine

Super-fine

colour

Colour is a great source of inspiration for the creative knitter. Try bold and vibrant colours together for a striking look, or a more sophisticated palette of natural, muted colours. Choose slabs of solid colour, or experiment with many different shades. You can use several colours of a plain yarn to introduce colour into your knitting, or you can use multi-coloured yarns instead. These are easier to use, since there is no joining in of new colours or sewing in of ends. 'Multi-coloured yarn' is a general term that I have used throughout this book to describe yarns that are dyed in many colours. Within this general heading are several types of multi-coloured yarn, some of which are shown on this swatch.

Self-striping wool yarn

Ribbon yarn

Short-pile eyelash yarn

Tweed yarn

Long-pile eyelash yarn

Striped yarn

Self-striping wool yarn (*shown twice 'cos it's so nice!*)

A GUIDE TO COLOUR

From top to bottom, the yarns illustrated right are described below:

Self-striping wool yarn has a long length of a colour that slowly merges into the next. These lengths are usually sufficient to knit a couple of rows. I used this for the Over the Rainbow Scarf (pages 22–23) and for the Full of Fun mittens (pages 40–41). For the scarf, I used two balls of the same colour but started each in a different place in the colour sequence. For the mittens, I used one ball and let the colours emerge as they were knitted. I also used this yarn for the Mighty Mitred Squares (pages 84–87), where each colour emerged to work a different shape and produce the patchwork effect.

Ribbon yarn has shorter lengths of colour that produce splashes of colour rather than stripes. The splashes are long enough to knit several stitches but not a complete row. I used one of these for the Simply Slinky Scarf (pages 26–27).

Short-pile eyelash yarn also has short splashes of colour that are further merged through the texture of the yarn.

Tweed yarn is a marl of two or more colours with flecks of contrasting colours. Using tweed yarn introduces depth of colour to any knitted fabric. This one is a twist of a blue-green ply with a turquoise ply. The flecks are purple and further shades of green. I have used several tweed yarns in the projects; for example, the Winter Warmer Scarf (page 77) has a lovely deep red tweed that introduces more colours into the fabric. The swatch for the Making Waves Wrap (page 57) uses a rich purple tweed.

Long-pile eyelash yarn has a jade-green strand twisted with a blue strand. The eyelash pile fluffs out from these core strands. A metallic thread is woven in to complete the impression of randomly placed colours.

Striped yarn is designed to be used for small pieces of knitting, such as socks, and produces a strict stripe pattern. Each colour is separated by a dark blue stripe so each is clearly defined. No colour merges with the next. You could break up the sequence by using two balls and working two rows with each ball, or by using two strands together to produce a marl yarn.

1 Astrakhan

2 Bouclé

3 Chenille

4 Cord

5 Eyelash

6 Matte cotton

texture

Yarns are available in a wide range of textures, from plain, plied yarns to extravagant concoctions of ribbon, bouclé or eyelash. I made these fantastic tassels to illustrate the diversity of yarn textures. Each one shows the qualities of the yarn and what type of fabric it makes when knitted. A simple stockinette stitch reveals how fabulous the yarns are; small patterned stitches would be lost in the texture, but how about trying a really chunky cable worked in the astrakhan or a frivolous lace stitch worked in the mohair?

A GUIDE TO TEXTURE

From top to bottom, the yarns used to make these tassels are described below:

1 Astrakhan yarn has a texture of loose snarls that curl across the surface of the fabric. Use a simple reverse stockinette stitch to display its texture fully.

2 Bouclé has a similar looped texture to astrakhan, formed when a loosely spun strand is allowed to wrap around itself into snarls and snags. This cotton bouclé is crisp and produces a dense texture like that of a towel. Softer bouclés in mohair and wool make a luxurious, deep fabric.

3 Chenille is a short-pile yarn that produces a wonderfully rich velvety fabric. This chunky version would be great on its own; a thinner chenille would add softness and luxury into a yarn mix (see Good Things Come in Threes, pages 48–53).

8 Metallic

7 Mercerized cotton

10 Ribbon

9 Mohair

11 Tape

12 Tweed

4 Cord is a smooth, round yarn. When knitted, each stitch sits apart from its neighbours, producing an open fabric. This is great for clearly defined knit and purl fabrics, and would add structure to a softer yarn mix (see Summer Scorcher Scarf, page 76).

5 Eyelash yarn looks like a frayed ribbon. Available in width from narrow to outrageously wide, it knits up into a fabric of deep shimmering waves. Add it to more demure yarns like a plain wool for a striking contrast (see Funky Fur Mittens, pages 42–43).

6 Matte cotton has a lovely dry texture; it has weight and will add strength and structure to a yarn mix. The colour of this cotton/silk mix is attractively dusty, like painted plaster.

7 Mercerized cotton is a tight, lustrous yarn that makes a very clean and crisp fabric. It is available in a wide range of bright, intense colours.

8 Metallic yarns are crunchy, modern and full of light. This is a mix of viscose and metallic elements that adds a sharp highlight to a soft fluid fabric. Add to any yarn mix for instant glamour (see Good Things Come in Threes, pages 48–53) or as a cheeky stripe (see Shake Your Pompoms Ski Hat, pages 70–73).

9 Mohair is a soft fluffy yarn; the fibres trap air and light to produce a feather-soft fabric. Use it on its own for a barely-there fabric or mix it with heavier yarns to add a haze of colour.

10 Ribbon is a woven version of tape. It is flat and varies in width from narrow to wide, and is available in any fibre from wool to synthetics. This ladder ribbon has a strong structure punctuated with sharp stabs of precise colour. Ribbons can be multi-coloured, stranded with metallic, open or solid structures, fluffy or crisp, slinky or hard (see All Wrapped Up, pages 24–25).

11 Tape is a fluid knitted flat yarn that rarely produces a completely flat fabric; it twists and folds on your needles. It folds in half for one stitch and then opens out for the next. This cotton version makes a fabric with structure, but a viscose version produces a wonderfully slinky fabric (see Simply Slinky Scarf, pages 26–27).

12 Tweed yarn is a combination of two or more colours, spun together or introduced as slubs or knots of colour. A knitted tweed fabric looks warm, cosy and resilient. You can contrast it with metallic or cotton for an exciting twist. Pure wool tweed makes fantastic fulled fabric; the colours merge into a dense brushed fabric (see Knitted Flowers, page 121).

needles

NEEDLE SIZES	
US	**Metric**
0	2mm
1	2.25mm
	2.5mm
2	2.75mm
	3mm
3	3.25mm
4	3.5mm
5	3.75mm
6	4mm
7	4.5mm
8	5mm
9	5.5mm
10	6mm
10½	6.5mm
	7mm
	7.5mm
11	8mm
13	9mm
15	10mm
17	12.75mm
19	15mm
35	19mm
	20mm

gauge

At the beginning of every project, I have given the gauge (tension) that you need to achieve to make the project successfully. The gauge is the number of stitches and rows you need to make 1in (2.5cm). This is a very important part of knitting: if you do not obtain the correct gauge, the garment will not be the correct size. This is especially important when you are knitting a project that needs to fit well, such as gloves and hats.

GAUGE MEASUREMENTS

The gauge is given over 4in (10cm). For example: the gauge for a light-weight (DK) yarn is 22 stitches and 28 rows to 4in (10cm) measured over stockinette stitch on size 6 (4mm) needles. To check your gauge, you must work a square of fabric measuring at least 6in (15cm), using the stated yarn, needle size and stitch. You can then measure the fabric in the middle of the square, avoiding the edge stitches, which will be distorted.

Sometimes it is difficult to achieve both the correct stitch and row count. It is more important to obtain the correct stitch count, so concentrate on achieving that. The row count matters only in projects such as the gloves, mittens and hats, where I have given shaping instructions over a certain number of rows. In a project where I have just given a length to work to, such as scarves and ponchos, the row count is not so important.

KNITTING A GAUGE SQUARE

To knit a gauge square in stockinette stitch, cast on the number of stitches stated for 4in (10cm) plus half as many again. For example: 22 sts plus 11 sts.

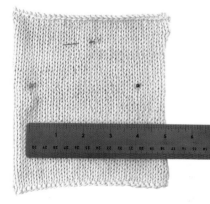

1 Work in stockinette stitch for 6in (15cm) and then bind off loosely.
2 Steam or wet press the square in the way that you will use for your finished project (see page 116). The information on the ball band will tell you whether you can steam the yarn or not.

3 Lay the square on a flat surface without stretching it. Place a ruler horizontally on the square and place a pin 1in (2.5cm) in from the edge and place another at 4in (10cm) from the first pin.
4 Do the same for the rows by placing the ruler vertically, keeping away from the cast-on and bound-off edges, which may pull the fabric in.
5 Count the number of stitches and rows between the pins: this is your gauge. If you have more stitches than the suggested number, your stitches are too small; you will need to use a size larger needle to make the stitches bigger and so obtain fewer stitches to 4in (10cm). If you have too few stitches, this means your stitches are too big; you need to use a size smaller needle to make the stitches smaller and so obtain more to 4in (10cm).
6 Work another square until you achieve the gauge stated in the pattern.

MEASURING TEXTURED YARNS

If you are using a textured yarn, it can be difficult to see individual stitches and rows. For yarns with a long pile, such as the faux fur shown, measure the 4in (10cm) for stitches and rows, placing a marker in a contrasting yarn. Leave long ends on these markers so they are visible through the long pile. Hold the square up to a window or a light (protect your eyes against a strong light). This will show up the stitches and rows clearly for you to count.

With yarns that are heavily textured, such as the bouclé shown, or a thick fleece or plush yarn, the stitches close up and make a uniform surface when knitted. Knit a contrasting coloured sewing cotton in with the yarn. This will show up the stitches and rows and make counting easier. Mark the 4in (10cm) for stitches and rows with a contrasting thread, so you can pull the fabric to make out difficult stitches without losing any pins.

It is often easier to make out the stitches and rows on the wrong side of the square, on the reverse stockinette side, so use this side to measure over.

If you are not sure what the individual stitches and rows look like, refer to page 105.

MEASURING OVER A STITCH PATTERN

If the gauge is quoted over a stitch pattern like that used for the Making Waves Scarf (see pages 54–57), cast on enough stitches to work complete repeats. The repeat of the pattern follows the asterisk; cast on a multiple of this number of stitches plus any stitches given at the beginning and end of the row.

USING GAUGE FOR SUBSTITUTING YARNS

For all these projects, I have suggested other yarns to use or different weights of yarn to mix up into a unique yarn. It is very important to keep aiming for the stated gauge when you alter the yarn mix, or the project will not be the correct size and the finished fabric may be too loose or too tight.

abbreviations

All knitting patterns include instructions that are abbreviated for the sake of brevity. The list here applies to the abbreviations that you will encounter to make the projects in this book.

alt	alternate
approx	approximately
beg	begin/beginning
cm	centimetre(s)
cont	continue
dec(s)	decrease(s)/decreasing
DK	double knitting
foll	following
g	gram
g st	garter stitch (k every row)
in(s)	inch(es)
inc(s)	increase(s)/increasing
k	knit
k2tog	knit 2 stitches together (1 stitch decreased)
k3tog	knit 3 stitches together (2 stitches decreased)
k3tog tbl	knit 3 stitches together through back of loops (2 sts decreased)
Kf&b	knit into the front and back (increase 1 stitch)
m	metre(s)
mm	millimetre(s)
M1	make one (increase 1 stitch)
oz	ounces
p	purl
patt(s)	pattern(s)
PB	place bead
PM	place marker
p2tog	purl 2 stitches together (1 stitch decreased)
p3tog	purl 3 stitches together (2 stitches decreased)
p3tog tbl	purl 3 stitches together through back of loops (2 stitches decreased)

rem	remain/ing
rep(s)	repeat(s)
rev st st	reverse stockinette stitch (1 row p, 1 row k) (UK: reverse stocking stitch)
RH	right hand
rnd(s)	round(s)
RS	right side
sl2tog-k1-psso	slip 2 stitches together, knit 1 stitch, pass 2 slipped stitches over (2 stitches decreased)
ssk	slip 2 stitches one at a time, knit 2 slipped stitches together (1 stitch decreased)
ssp	slip 2 stitches one at a time, purl 2 slipped stitches together through the back of the loops (1 stitch decreased)
sl	slip
sl 1	slip 1 stitch
st(s)	stitch(es)
st st	stockinette stitch (1 row k, 1 row p) (UK: stocking stitch)
tbl	through back of loop
tog	together
WS	wrong side
yd(s)	yard(s)
yfwd	yarn forward
yo	yarn over
*	repeat directions following * as many times as indicated or until end of row
[ ]	instructions in square brackets refer to larger sizes
( )	repeat instructions in round brackets the number of times

In the instructions for the projects, I have favoured US knitting terms. Refer to this box if you need a translation.

US TERM	UK TERM
stockinette stitch	stocking stitch
reverse stockinette stitch	reverse stocking stitch
seed stitch	moss stitch
moss stitch	double moss stitch
bind off	cast off
gauge	tension

reading knitting patterns

A knitting pattern tells you how to knit and make up a knitted project. The instructions use shorthand phrases and abbreviations, otherwise they would be far too long. The abbreviations appear in a list on page 16, with an explanation of what they mean. Many are commonly used, such as k and p. Others refer to special stitches, like C4F. These are explained in the pattern and in the technique section at the back of this book (see page 112 for further instructions on working with cables).

SIZES

Some of the knitting patterns are written in more than one size. Items such as hats, gloves and mittens need to be in different sizes to ensure that they fit you well, whereas garments such as the scarves and ponchos are one size for everyone. You can choose which size will fit you best by looking at the measurements section of the pattern. Here, each size will have a measurement for length and width, or for head circumference. Choose the size closest to your own measurements. In the written instructions, the smallest size is given first (outside the brackets) and the remaining sizes are inside the square brackets, separated by colons. For example, the gloves can be knitted in S [M: L] sizes; small, medium and large. Your size will always appear in the same place in the bracket; instructions for the first size will always be first, for the second size they will be second, and so on.

READING SIZE INSTRUCTIONS

Square brackets are also used within the instructions to indicate the number of stitches and rows to be worked, or how many times a pattern is repeated, for each size. For example, cast on 30 [32:34] sts, or work 2 [4:6] rows. If a zero appears for your size, do not work the instruction it is referring to. For example, repeat 1 [0:1] times. If only one figure appears then it refers to all sizes. Read through the pattern and underline or highlight your size in the square brackets.

CABLE OR PATTERN PANELS

In some projects, such as the Classic Cabled Poncho (pages 96–99) and the Love-heart Gloves (pages 82–83), I have put instructions for the cable or pattern panels outside the main project instructions. This is because these panels would make the project instructions very long and complicated, and a lot of information would be repeated. The panel is set within a group of stitches; keep following the pattern panel while working your way through the project instructions. For example:
Row 1 (P1, k1) twice, k5, work 1st row of panel A, k5, work 1st row of panel B, k5, work 1st row of panel C, k5, (k1, p1) twice.

IMPERIAL AND METRIC MEASUREMENTS

The patterns are written in both imperial (inches and ounces) and metric (centimetres and grams) measurements. Stick to one or the other; some imperial to metric measurements are not exact conversions.

COMMON SHORTHAND PHRASES

cont as set instead of repeating the same instructions over and over, you must continue to work as previously told. For example: cont to inc 4 sts as set on next and every foll alt round.
keeping patt correct continue with a stitch pattern, keeping it correctly worked over the correct number of stitches, while doing something that may interfere with the stitch pattern. For example: keeping heart motif panel correct, cont in st st.
work as given for to avoid repeating instructions. For example: the left glove is worked the same as the right glove to a certain point, usually indicated by asterisks.
* repeat directions following * as many times as indicated or until end of row. For example: *p2, yo, (p1, yo, p1) into next st, yo, p2, p2tog, p3tog, p2tog; rep from * once more.
( ) repeat instructions in round brackets the number of times indicated. For example: (k12, k3tog) twice.

Complicated instructions, such as those required for cable panels, are listed separately from the main instructions of a project.

and now to knit...

gorgeous
garter stitch

You can create individual and exciting items without using complicated techniques or investing a lot of time. The following three projects use perhaps the simplest technique of all: they are all worked in garter stitch, which means that you knit every row. There is no pattern to learn, so these projects are ideal for beginners. Here, it is the choice of yarn that gives the scarves their visual impact. Take these projects as a starting point for your own inspiration: it is easy to adapt each one for a different yarn, to alter the size, or to add embellishments.

A simple stitch is often the best way to show off a beautiful variegated yarn – the one used here features a rainbow array of colours and a cosily lush texture. Anything more complicated might have made the gloriously rich colours of this tasselled scarf look too fussy. See pages 22–23.

The deep colours and funky sparkle of this unique yarn are shown off to their full advantage in this glamorous wrap – just the thing when you want to be chic for a special evening out, or to add some glitz to your everyday wardrobe. See pages 24–25.

Here, garter stitch has been used to create a chic and colourful scarf from a drapey ribbon yarn. The light, slinky weight of this yarn and its fun, vibrant colours make it the perfect accessory to liven up a summer outfit. See pages 26–27.

over the rainbow scarf

MEASUREMENTS
5½in (13cm) wide by 64in (162cm) long
(excluding tassels)

GATHER TOGETHER...
materials
2 x 3½oz/100g hanks of bulky-weight (chunky)
multi-coloured wool/silk mix yarn (131yd/120m
per hank) in orange/green mix

needles and notions
1 pair of size 10½ (7mm) needles
Piece of cardboard 9in (23cm) wide
Size H/8 (5mm) crochet hook

GAUGE
14 sts and 24 rows to 4in (10cm) measured
over garter stitch (every row k) using size
10½ (7mm) needles

YARN FOCUS
This 'striped' scarf is made super-easy by using
two balls of multi-coloured wool yarn of the same
shade number. This yarn features long lengths of
colour that are enough to knit two or three rows.
I used one ball that started with pink and another
ball that started with brown and knitted them in
two-row stripes. The colour mix for each ball is the
same, but by using two balls that begin in different
places in the colour sequence, a fantastic random
stripe effect is created. For the specific yarn
details for all of the projects featured in this book,
see pages 125–126.

Garter stitch is an ideal stitch to use for scarves because it looks the same
from both sides (there is no 'wrong' and 'right' side), and it lies nice and flat
instead of curling in at the edges. Garter-stitch scarves are great projects for
beginners because you use only one stitch – you simply knit each row – and
there is no shaping to worry about. Just because these items are simple
to make doesn't mean that they are boring, however – inspire yourself by
experimenting with stunning colour combinations, as we have here.

Knit your scarf...
Label one ball A and the other ball B.
Using size 10½ (7mm) needles and A, cast on 18
sts loosely and knit 2 rows.
Join in B and knit 2 rows.
Bring A in front of B and knit 2 rows with A.
Bring B in front of A and knit 2 rows with B.
Cont in garter stitch, working 2 rows in A then 2
rows in B, always bringing the new yarn in front of
the old at the beg of the row to keep the edge neat,
until scarf measures 64in (162cm) long.
Bind off loosely.

to finish...
Wrap the yarn loosely around the piece of
cardboard. Cut the wrapped strands at the bottom
and remove the cardboard. Take two lengths of yarn
and fold in half. Using the crochet hook, pull the
strands through the edge of the scarf from front to
back by catching the fold with the hook. Pass the
ends through the folded loop and pull to tighten
the knot. Space each bunch of strands evenly
along the edge.

*The tasselled fringe adds
a pleasing embellishment
to this scarf.*

new yarn, new look!

You can use any yarn to knit a basic scarf. Just check on the ball band for the number of stitches to 4in (10cm). Decide on the finished width of the scarf and divide this measurement by 4in (10cm); for example, a 6in (15cm)-wide scarf would need one and a half times the stitch number, whereas a scarf 12in (30cm) wide would need three times the stitch number. For this pretty blue scarf, I used a soft medium-weight (aran) velour yarn. It could be worn in summer as well as winter. I have added a border of two sizes of shell buttons; you could use a wider selection of buttons to match your yarn (see Smart Girl Gloves on pages 58–61 for ideas).

IN THE MIX
Medium-weight (aran) velour-style tape (100% nylon – 63yd/58m per ball) in variegated blue

DESIGN NOTE
Sewing on buttons are a fun way of adding detail and interest to the edges of a scarf. Choose ones that tone in with the yarn for an elegant look, or go for a mix of colours, textures and sizes for a lively, quirky effect.

AND IT DOESN'T END THERE…
Garter stitch is such a simple fabric to produce that it is ideal for experimenting with yarns. You could use yarns of two different textures but in similar shades for the stripes – how about a mohair with a tweed wool, or a crisp cotton with a soft chenille? Work two contrasting colours together; pink and green always fizzes with energy. Otherwise, try natural autumnal shades such as bronze and russet.

all wrapped up

MEASUREMENTS
11in (28cm) wide by 56in (142cm) long

GATHER TOGETHER...
materials
9 x 1¾oz/50g hanks of bulky-weight (chunky) multi-coloured nylon ribbon with metallic core (66yd/60m per hank) in purple/red/gold mix

needles and notions
1 pair of size 11 (8mm) needles

GAUGE
13 sts and 22 rows to 4in (10cm) measured over garter stitch (every row k) using size 11 (8mm) needles

YARN FOCUS
This is one of those yarns that you just have to buy when you see it, with no thought as to what you might use it for. It is a wide ribbon in shades of red, purple and orange with a metallic gold thread running through it. Such a special yarn can be knitted simply without complicated stitches or shaping. It is enough just to produce a length of fabulous fabric to drape around you.

If you can make a scarf, you can make a wrap – just cast on more stitches to obtain the necessary width of fabric to keep your shoulders as well as your neck covered. Wraps are just the thing to show off a spectacular yarn – they are simple, stylish and glamorous.

Knit your wrap...
Using size 11 (8mm) needles, cast on 40 sts loosely and work in garter stitch until wrap measures 56in (142cm) long.
Bind off loosely.

to finish...
Sew in all ends neatly.

DESIGN SECRETS UNRAVELLED...
There are so many desirable yarns around that it can be hard to know where to start. Fun or faux fur yarns in natural shades or vibrant colours make a fantastic wrap for winter. Imagine snuggling down into the depths of a luxurious wrap while the rest of the world freezes! Or you could use an eyelash yarn in dramatic shades for a softer, slinkier look for evening. A delicate silk yarn would make a special wrap for a wedding or other special occasions, while a natural-dyed, hand-spun yarn would be really individual.

The ribbon-like nature of this yarn works well in garter stitch, combining simplicity with some textural interest.

simply slinky scarf

MEASUREMENTS
2¼in (5.5cm) wide by 92in (233cm) long

GATHER TOGETHER...
materials
4 x 1¾oz (50g) hanks of medium-weight (aran)
viscose tape (68yd/62m per hank), multi-coloured

needles and notions
1 pair of size 10½ (7mm) needles
Piece of cardboard as wide as desired fringe
Size H/8 (5mm) crochet hook

GAUGE
18 sts and 25 rows to 4in (10cm) measured over
garter stitch (every row k) using size 10½/7mm
needles

YARN FOCUS

I wanted this scarf to have drape, to be very slinky
and to be weighty enough not to slip around too
much. The yarn I chose is a knitted tape made
from viscose. This type of yarn is flat instead of
round and so produces a textured fabric even when
knitted in stockinette stitch. Viscose is a plant fibre
and is often used in yarns to add shine or a satin-
like quality.

The appeal of this scarf lies both in its slinky, elegant drape and its fabulous
rainbow colours. Even with a simple knitting technique, such as garter stitch,
you can produce a dazzling many-coloured fabric using multi-dyed yarns. The
key to using such yarns is to work with two balls at once. Knit two rows with ball
A, then two rows with ball B. Knitting from one ball will produce blocks of colour,
but using two balls will interrupt these colour blocks with a flash of another
colour. A fabric knitted like this will have no sequence of colours; it will be totally
random and spontaneous.

Knit your scarf...

Label one ball A and the other ball B.
Using size 10½ (7mm) needles and A,
cast on 10 sts loosely and knit 2 rows.
Join in B and knit 2 rows.
Bring A in front of B and knit 2 rows with A.
Bring B in front of A and knit 2 rows with B.
Cont in garter stitch, working 2 rows in A then
2 rows in B, always bringing the new yarn in front of
the old at the beg of the row to keep the edge neat,
until scarf measures 92in (233cm) long.
Bind off loosely.

to finish...

Sew in all ends neatly. Note that a knitted tape yarn
will do what your knitting does if not bound off – it
will unravel. To stop this happening, tie a small knot
close to the end of each strand and cut the ends
at an angle once you have woven them in. Use
sewing thread to sew this into the fabric to make
doubly sure. Wrap the yarn loosely around a piece
of cardboard the required length of the fringe. Cut
the wrapped strands at the bottom and remove
the cardboard. Fold two lengths in half and, using
the crochet hook, pull the strands through from the
front to the back by catching the fold with the hook.
Pass the ends through the folded loop and pull
to tighten the knot. Space each bunch of strands
evenly along the edge. Knot the ends of the fringe
to prevent them from unravelling.

*The unique construction
of knitted tape yarns
lends this fabric its
fabulous drape.*

heads up
hat

Hats are the perfect project when you want a quick knitting fix – they don't take long to make, and are both stylish and practical additions to your wardrobe. This is such a simple hat to knit and wear that you will want to make several. It hugs the head and can be worn low over your ears in winter or as a fashion statement on milder days. You can add the flower or leave it plain. Pin on a fabric flower, a brooch or sew on a sequin trim for a bit of sparkle.

The knitted petals add a delightfully feminine touch to this simply chic hat.

DESIGN SECRETS UNRAVELLED…

It is important to use the right yarn when you are knitting hats. Think about the look you want to achieve. If you want a hat to pull on in the winter when warmth and function are the main priorities, then choose a tweed wool or oiled wool to repel water. If you want a lighter hat for fashion rather than practical reasons, then how about a crisp mercerized cotton in a bright colour or a jazzy metallic mix yarn? Alternatively, you could go back to nature with a linen or hemp yarn. Try working the flower embellishment in a contrasting colour and fill the centre with beads and sequins or a large button.

YARN FOCUS

I wanted a very soft, light yarn for this hat, to give warmth without weight. Mohair was ideal, as the hairs lock in warm air. I also wanted a light-weight (DK) yarn so the fabric wouldn't be too thick and the stitches so big that any shaping would be too obvious. If I had used a finer yarn, the hat would have been too thin and not kept its shape when worn.

heads up hat

MEASUREMENTS
Will stretch to fit head circumference 20 [22]in (51 [56]cm)

GATHER TOGETHER...
materials
2 x ⅞oz/25g balls of light-weight (DK) mohair yarn (150yd/138m per ball) in soft mauve

needles
1 pair of size 3 (3.25mm) needles
1 pair of size 6 (4mm) needles

GAUGE
24 sts and 30 rows to 4in (10cm) measured over st st (1 row k, 1 row p) on size 6 (4mm) needles

This cute and versatile hat is shaped so it fits you snugly – it's both chic and cosy. Start with a thin band of k1, p1 rib and then simply work in stockinette stitch until reaching the crown. This is shaped with k2tog and p2tog (see page 110). The petals are shaped using k2tog and yfwd as well as ssk and sl2tog-k1-psso (see pages 110–111).

Knit your hat...
Using size 3 (3.25mm) needles, cast on 122 [134] sts.
Row 1 *K1, p1; rep from * to end.
Rep until rib measures 1in (2.5cm).
Change to size 6 (4mm) needles and cont in st st (1 row k, 1 row p), beg with a k row, until work measures 5½in (14cm) from beg, ending with a p row.

Shape crown
Dec Row K1, (k2tog, k8 [9]) 12 times, k1. 110 [122] sts.
Work 3 rows.
Dec Row K1, (k2tog, k7 [8]) 12 times, k1. 98 [110] sts.
Work 1 row.
Dec Row K1, (k2tog, k6 [7]) 12 times, k1. 86 [98] sts.
Work 1 row.
Dec Row K1, (k2tog, k5 [6]) 12 times, k1. 74 [86] sts.
Work 1 row.
Dec Row K1, (k2tog, k4 [5]) 12 times, k1. 62 [74] sts.
Dec Row P4 [5], p2tog, (p3 [4], p2tog) 11 times, p1. 50 [62] sts.
Dec Row K1, (k2tog, k2 [3]) 12 times, k1. 38 [50] sts.
Dec Row P2 [3], p2tog, (p1 [2], p2tog) 11 times, p1. 26 [38] sts.
Dec Row K1, (k3tog) 8 [12] times, k1. 10 [14] sts.
Cut yarn and thread through rem sts. Pull up tight and fasten off.

knit your flower...
Petals (make 5)
Using size 3 (3.25mm) needles, cast on 3 sts and p 1 row.
Row 1 RS K1, (yfwd, k1) twice. 5 sts.
Row 2 and every foll WS row P to end.
Row 3 K2, yfwd, k1, yfwd, k2. 7 sts.
Row 5 K3, yfwd, k1, yfwd, k3. 9 sts.
Row 7 K4, yfwd, k1, yfwd, k4. 11 sts.
Row 9 K5, yfwd, k1, yfwd, k5. 13 sts.
Row 11 Ssk, k9, k2tog. 11 sts.
Row 13 Ssk, k7, k2tog. 9 sts.
Row 15 Ssk, k5, k2tog. 7 sts.
Row 17 Ssk, k3, k2tog. 5 sts.
Row 19 Ssk, k1, k2tog. 3 sts.
Row 21 Sl2tog-k1-psso.
Cut yarn, leaving a long tail for sewing up.

to finish...
Sew in all ends on hat. Press all pieces according to instructions on ball band. Sew the five petals onto the hat in a circle to form a flower. Join back seam of hat.

new yarn, new look!

I tried two variations here; the first is for a beautiful light hat with a rose detail. Knitting anything in fine-weight (4ply) yarns takes time, but don't overlook them for quicker-to-knit yarns; this wonderfully deep, rich red tweed makes a fantastic fabric. By using two strands together, I made the light-weight (DK) yarn that I needed for this version of the basic hat. Add some softness with a pink rose worked in light-weight (DK) mohair yarn (see page 121 for instructions on how to make the flower). The second variation uses a multi-coloured knitted tape yarn; these are great for adding colours without the extra work of changing yarns. Add a border of beads along the cast-on edge. Sew them on, being careful not to pull too tightly; the cast-on edge needs to stretch around your head. Alternate single beads with picots of four beads. To make a picot, thread three beads onto your yarn, pull up against the rib, then take your needle back through the second bead. Thread on a fourth bead and secure to the rib.

IN THE MIX

HAT WITH ROSE
A Fine-weight (4ply) tweed wool yarn (100% wool – 162yd/90m per ball) in red
B Light-weight (DK) mohair yarn (70% super kid mohair/25% nylon/5% wool – 150yd/138m per ball) in soft pink

HAT WITH BEADS
Light-weight (DK) multi-coloured yarn (100% soy silk™ – 240yd/220m per ball) in shades of pink, lilac and purple

smitten mittens

Mittens are simple and inspiring projects; they are also the easiest way to start knitting gloves. We set out five ideas here to get you going. The plain and embroidered mittens are written for a medium-weight (aran) yarn (pictured opposite). On pages 36–43 are three more fantastic styles: the striped mittens are knitted in light-weight (DK) yarn; the fabulous pink mittens use a thicker fashion yarn; and the felted mittens have a lovely dense texture. All of them are worked in stockinette stitch and four have a snug-fitting cuff in k1, p1 rib. The thumb on each mitten is shaped using M1 (see page 108), and the tops are decreased with ssk and k2tog (see page 110).

DESIGN SECRETS UNRAVELLED…

You could create a great mix of yarns for these mittens. Use two light-weight (DK) yarns; one wool, the other a textured yarn. Mix colours together; brights or naturals, icy shades or hot pinks. Add a metallic silver yarn to a soft white mohair for a snowy sparkle, or mix in a luxury yarn like cashmere for extra snugness. Keep in mind that you are aiming for a final combination that will knit up to a medium-weight (aran) gauge.

YARN FOCUS

For these two sets of mittens, I chose medium-weight (aran) wool yarns so they are quick to knit when the first snowflakes start falling. The hand-dyed multi-coloured yarn makes the mittens funky and totally individual.

The simple shape of the plain mittens is perfect to show off the unique colour mix of this hand-dyed yarn, while the bold single colour of the embroidered mittens makes the ideal background for the pretty stitched detail.

simple mittens

MEASUREMENTS
To fit sizes S [M:L]; width around palm is 7
[7½:8]in (18 [19:20.5]cm) and 7 [7½:8]in (18
[19:20.5]cm) long from wrist

GATHER TOGETHER...
materials
1 x 3½oz (100g) hank of medium-weight (aran)
multi-coloured wool yarn (150yd/138m per hank)
in pink/green/gold/ecru mix

needles
1 pair of size 5 (3.75mm) needles
1 pair of size 7 (4.5mm) needles

GAUGE
18 sts and 24 rows to 4in (10cm) measured over
st st (1 row k, 1 row p) using size 7 (4.5mm)
needles

Here is a simple pair of mittens made extraordinary because of the gorgeous yarn. Cast on the cuff loosely and work in k1, p1 rib on the smaller needles. The thumb gusset is increased out and the thumb is worked separately; it's not as difficult as it looks. From then on it's simple stockinette stitch until you reach the top shaping. Complete this pair of mittens and you'll be eager to start the next pair – embellished by some beautiful embroidery.

Knit your right mitten...
Using size 5 (3.75mm) needles, cast on 32
[34:36] sts loosely.
Row 1 *K1, p1; rep from * to end.
Rep this row until rib measures 2in (5cm).
Change to size 7 (4.5mm) needles.
Work 2 rows in st st (1 row k, 1 row p), starting with
a k row.**

Shape thumb gusset
Next Row K16 [17:18], M1, k2, M1, k14 [15:16].
34 [36:38] sts.
Work 3 rows in st st.
Next Row K16 [17:18], M1, k4, M1, k14 [15:16].
36 [38:40] sts.
Work 3 rows in st st.
Next Row K16 [17:18], M1, k6, M1, k14 [15:16].
38 [40:42] sts.
Work 3 rows in st st.
Next Row K16 [17:18], M1, k8, M1, k14 [15:16].
40 [42:44] sts.
Purl 1 row.

Thumb
Next Row K26 [27:28] and turn.
Next Row Cast on 2 sts (using the cable cast-on
– see page 103), p12 (including 2 sts just cast on),
turn and cast on 2 sts.
***Work 2½ [2¾:3]in (6 [7:7.5]cm) on these 14
sts only for thumb, ending with a p row. Measure
the knitting next to your thumb, placing the cast-on
sts at the base of your thumb. You may need to add
or subtract rows here to fit your thumb length.

Next Row K1, (k2tog, k1) 4 times, k1. 10 sts.
P 1 row.
Next Row K1, (k2tog) 4 times, k1. 6 sts.
Cut yarn and thread through rem sts. Pull up tight
and fasten off. Join thumb seam.
With RS of work facing and using size 7 (4.5mm)
needles, pick up and knit 2 sts across base of
thumb, k across 14 [15:16] unworked sts on
left-hand needle. 32 [34:36] sts.
****Cont in st st across all sts until mitten
measures 5½ [6:6½]in (14 [15:16.5]cm) from
top of rib, ending with a p row. Try the mitten on;
it should be approx 1½in (4cm) below the top
of your longest finger. You may need to add or
subtract rows here to fit your hand length.

Shape top
Next Row (K1, ssk, k10 [11:12], k2tog, k1) twice.
28 [30:32] sts.
P 1 row.
Next Row (K1, ssk, k8 [9:10], k2tog, k1) twice. 24
[26:28] sts.
P1 row.
Next Row (K1, ssk, k6 [7:8], k2tog, k1) twice. 20
[22:24] sts.
P1 row.
Next Row *(K1, k2tog) 3 [3:4] times, k1 [2:0]; rep
from * once more. 14 [16:16] sts.
P1 row.
Next Row *K1, (k2tog) 3 times, k0 [1:1]; rep from
* once more.
Cut yarn and draw through rem 8 [10:10] sts.

knit your left mitten...

Work as given for right mitten to **.

Shape thumb gusset

Next Row K14 [15:16], M1, k2, M1, k16 [17:18].
34 [36:38] sts.
Work 3 rows in st st.
Next Row K14 [15:16], M1, k4, M1, k16 [17:18].
36 [38:40] sts.
Work 3 rows in st st.
Next Row K14 [15:16], M1, k6, M1, k16 [17:18].
38 [40:42] sts.
Work 3 rows in st st.
Next Row K14 [15:16], M1, k8, M1, k16 [17:18].
40 [42:44] sts.
Purl 1 row.

Thumb

Next Row K24 [25:26] and turn.
Next Row Cast on 2 sts (using the cable cast-on),
p12 (including 2 sts just cast on), turn and cast on
2 sts.
Complete as given for thumb of right mitten
from ***.
With RS of work facing and using size 7 (4.5mm)
needles, pick up and knit 2 sts across base of
thumb, k across 16 [17:18] unworked sts on left-
hand needle. 32 [34:36] sts.
Work as given for right mitten from ****.

to finish...

Sew in all ends. Press all pieces according to
instructions on the ball band. Join side seams.

A plain pair of mittens is given added
zing with this bright embroidery.

They feature chain stitch and lazy daisy stitch (see
page 118). I wanted a dark colour to allow the
embroidery to shine. You need 2 x 1¾oz (50g)
balls of medium-weight (aran) alpaca/silk mix
yarn (71yd/65m per ball) in dark blue, and
oddments of light-weight (DK) wool in lime green
and bright pink. Knit the mittens as per the pattern
on page 34. Work the embroidery on the back of
each mitten as shown below. Use lazy daisy stitch
for flowers, chain stitch for the stems and a single
chain stitch filled with a straight stitch for the leaves.

DESIGN SECRETS UNRAVELLED...

Instead of light-weight (DK) yarn, try tapestry wool
or embroidery threads for the flower design. Silk
threads are extravagant, but fantastic! Try adding
beads or sequins to the centre of the flowers.
You could use a bright colour with a contrasting
dark embroidery, such as hot pink with dark green
stems and leaves and deep red flowers.

*Follow this
template to
embellish the
embroidered
mittens.*

striped mittens

These mittens (see pages 38–39) are made in light-weight (DK) yarn, which is thick enough to keep your hands warm while still being light and flexible. Because you need only small amounts of each colour, you could use tapestry wools instead. These are available in a far greater range of colours and knit up to light-weight (DK) gauge. Add a few of these and also any thinner crewel wools by using two strands together. If you don't want stripes, make up a light-weight (DK) yarn by using two fine-weight (4ply) yarns together.

full of fun mittens

Fulling these mittens (see pages 40–41) gives them a unique texture. Fabrics to be fulled are always knitted looser than normal. During fulling, the wool expands, and the fibres open up and mesh together so that individual stitches disappear. Multi-coloured yarn is beautiful when fulled because all the colours merge together. You could use a multi-coloured yarn with splashes of colour, or you could choose a tweed yarn with flecks of colour, which will sit in the fabric like dots. Test your yarn by fulling your gauge square.

funky fur mittens

You can create unique textures by combining a fashion yarn with a natural-fibre yarn (see pages 42–43). Eyelash yarns, ribbon yarns or metallic yarns could be mixed with plain wool, tweed wool or mohair. Yarns with longer hairs would make a fantastic fluffy pair of mittens, while shorter textures would allow the contrasting natural-fibre yarn to be seen.

Find out how to make all these fabulous mittens over the next few pages.

striped mittens

This pair of vibrantly colourful mittens is made from light-weight (DK) yarns worked in four-row stripes; remember to weave the ends in as you knit so there's no tedious sewing in when you've finished.

MEASUREMENTS

To fit sizes S [M:L]; width around palm is 7 [7½:8]in (18 [19:20.5]cm) and 7 [7½:8]in (18 [19:20.5]cm) long from wrist

GATHER TOGETHER...

materials

Oddments of light-weight (DK) yarns in at least 10 colours

needles

1 pair of size 3 (3.25mm) needles
1 pair of size 6 (4mm) needles

GAUGE

22 sts and 28 rows to 4in (10cm) measured over st st (1 row k, 1 row p) using size 6 (4mm) needles

knit note *Work in a stripe pattern of 4 rows throughout.*

Knit your right mitten...

Using size 3 (3.25mm) needles and first colour cast on 38 [40:44] sts loosely. Work in 4-row stripes throughout.
Row 1 *K1, p1; rep from * to end.
Rep this row until rib measures 2in (5cm).
Change to size 6 (4mm) needles, and working in st st (1 row k, 1 row p), work 2 rows.**

Shape thumb gusset

Next Row K19 [20:22], M1, k2, M1, k17 [18:20]. 40 [42:46] sts.
Work 3 rows in st st.
Next Row K19 [20:22], M1, k4, M1, k17 [18:20]. 42 [44:48] sts.
Work 3 rows in st st.
Next Row K19 [20:22], M1, k6, M1, k17 [18:20]. 44 [46:50] sts.
Work 3 rows in st st.
Next Row K19 [20:22], M1, k8, M1, k17 [18:20]. 46 [48:52] sts.
Work 3 rows in st st.
Next Row K19 [20:22], M1, k10, M1, k17 [18:20]. 48 [50:54] sts.
Purl 1 row.

Thumb

Next Row K31 [32:34] and turn.
Next Row Cast on 2 sts (using cable cast-on), p14 (including 2 sts just cast on), turn and cast on 2 sts.
***Work 2½ [2¾:3]in (6 [7:7.5]cm) on these 16 sts only for thumb, ending with a p row. Measure the knitting next to your thumb, placing the cast-on sts at the base of your thumb. You may need to add or subtract rows here to fit your thumb length.
Next Row K1, (k2tog, k1) 5 times. 11 sts.
P 1 row.
Next Row K1, (k2tog) 5 times. 6 sts.
Cut yarn and thread through rem sts. Pull up tight and fasten off. Join thumb seam.
With RS of work facing and using size 6 (4mm) needles, pick up and knit 2 sts across base of thumb, k across 17 [18:20] unworked sts on left-hand needle. 38 [40:44] sts.
****Cont in st st across all sts until mitten measures 5½ [6:6½]in (14 [16:18]cm) from top of rib, ending with a p row. Try the mitten on; it should be approx 1½in (4cm) below the top of your longest finger. You may need to add or subtract rows here to fit your hand length.

YARN FOCUS

This is a great way to use up your stash of light-weight (DK) yarns – all those ball ends and oddments that you've been saving for some project, some day. These mittens are knitted in a random pattern of four-row stripes. Go through your stash and pick out at least ten colours that go together. Place all your yarns into a bag. Pick out a new yarn without looking and knit one row with it. If it looks good, complete the four-row stripe. If it doesn't, don't pull back the work; simply pick up another yarn and complete the four-row stripe with this. Often the yarn you didn't like will look better when surrounded with other colours. If you still don't like it when the mitten has been completed, Swiss darn or embroider over it, or sew beads or sequins onto it. Working in this random way produces a unique and eye-catching set of mittens.

Shape top

Next Row (K1, ssk, k13 [14:16], k2tog, k1) twice. 34 [36:40] sts.

P 1 row.

Next Row (K1, ssk, k11 [12:14], k2tog, k1) twice. 30 [32:36] sts.

P1 row.

Next Row (K1, ssk, k9 [10:12], k2tog, k1) twice. 26 [28:32] sts.

P1 row.

Next Row (K1, ssk, k7 [8:10], k2tog, k1) twice. 22 [24:28] sts.

P1 row.

Next Row *K0 [1:1], (K1, k2tog) 3 [3:4] times, k2 [2:1]; rep from * once more. 16 [18:20] sts.

P1 row.

Next Row *K1, (k2tog) 3 [3:4] times, k1 [2:1]; rep from * once more.

Cut yarn and draw through rem 10 [12:12] sts.

knit your left mitten...

Work as given for right mitten to **.

Shape thumb gusset

Next Row K17 [18:20], M1, k2, M1, k19 [20:22]. 40 [42:46] sts.

Work 3 rows in st st.

Next Row K17 [18:20], M1, k4, M1, k19 [20:22]. 42 [44:48] sts.

Work 3 rows in st st.

Next Row K17 [18:20], M1, k6, M1, k19 [20:22]. 44 [46:50] sts.

Work 3 rows in st st.

Next Row K17 [18:20], M1, k8, M1, k19 [20:22]. 46 [48:52] sts.

Work 3 rows in st st.

Next Row K17 [18:20], M1, k10, M1, k19 [20:22]. 48 [50:54] sts.

Purl 1 row.

Thumb

Next Row K29 [30:32] and turn.

Next Row Cast on 2 sts (using cable cast-on), p14 (including 2 sts just cast on), turn and cast on 2 sts.

Complete as given for thumb of right mitten from ***.

With RS of work facing and using size 6 (4mm) needles, pick up and knit 2 sts across base of thumb, k across 19 [20:22] unworked sts on left hand needle. 38 [40:44] sts.

Work as given for right mitten from ****.

to finish...

Sew in all ends. Press all pieces according to instructions on the ball band. Join side seams.

Be bold with your choice of colours for these stripey mittens; some colour combinations that you would never usually consider can work brilliantly when used in this random way.

full of fun mittens

MEASUREMENTS

To fit sizes S [M:L]; width around palm is
7 [7½:8]in (18 [19:20.5]cm) and 7 [7½:8]in
(18 [19:20.5]cm) long from wrist (after fulling)

GATHER TOGETHER...
materials
2 x 1¾oz (50g) balls of bulky-weight (chunky)
wool multi-coloured yarn (109yd/100m per ball)
in blue/green mix

needles and notions
1 pair of size 9 (5.5mm) needles
Two appliqué motifs

GAUGE
Before fulling – 15 sts and 20 rows to 4in (10cm)
measured over st st (1 row k, 1 row p) using
size 9 (5.5mm) needles.
After fulling – 17 sts and 26 rows to 4in (10cm)

YARN FOCUS
Only a pure wool yarn or one with a high wool
content will full. I chose this multi-coloured 100%
wool yarn because it felts very easily and the
colour changes are fantastic.

Fulling a knitted fabric makes it thicker and therefore warmer; it also gives it a brushed appearance. I love the contrast of this with the sparkle and glamour of the sequin motif. You can wear the mittens with the cuff rolled up or down. When completed and before fulling, these mittens look quite strange; they will be very long and thin. This is because the fabric shrinks more in its length than in its width during fulling. See page 115 for fulling instructions.

Knit your right mitten...
Using size 9 (5.5mm) needles, cast on 30 [32:34]
sts loosely.
Work 16 rows in st st (1 row k, 1 row p), starting
with a k row.**

Shape thumb gusset
Next Row K15 [16:17], M1, k2, M1, k13 [14:15].
32 [34:36] sts.
Work 3 rows in st st.
Next Row K15 [16:17], M1, k4, M1, k13 [14:15].
34 [36:38] sts.
Work 3 rows in st st.
Next Row K15 [16:17], M1, k6, M1, k13 [14:15].
36 [38:40] sts.
Work 3 rows in st st.
Next Row K15 [16:17], M1, k8, M1, k13 [14:15].
38 [40:42] sts.
Work 3 rows in st st.
Next Row K15 [16:17], M1, k10, M1, k13 [14:15].
40 [42:44] sts.
Purl 1 row.

Thumb
Next Row K27 [28:29] and turn.
Next Row Cast on 2 sts (using cable cast-on),
p14 (including 2 sts just cast on), turn and cast
on 2 sts.
***Work 3 [3½:4]in (7.5 [9:10]cm) on these 16 sts
only for thumb, ending with a p row.
Next Row K1, (k2tog, k1) 5 times. 11 sts.
P 1 row.
Next Row K1, (k2tog) 5 times. 6 sts.
Cut yarn and thread through rem sts. Pull up tight
and fasten off. Join thumb seam.
With RS of work facing and using size 9 (5.5mm)
needles, pick up and knit 2 sts across base of
thumb, k across 13 [14:15] unworked sts on left
hand needle. 30 [32:34] sts.
****Cont in st st across all sts until mitten
measures 7 [7¾:8½]in (18 [19.5:21.5]cm) from
beg of thumb gusset, ending with a p row.

Shape top
Next Row (K1, ssk, k9 [10:11], k2tog, k1) twice. 26
[28:30] sts.
P 1 row.

Next Row (K1, ssk, k7 [8:9], k2tog, k1) twice.
22 [24:26] sts.
P 1 row.
Next Row (K1, ssk, k5 [6:7], k2tog, k1) twice.
18 [20:22] sts.
P 1 row.
Next Row *K1, k2tog; rep from * to last 0 [2:1] sts,
k0 [2:1]. 12 [14:15] sts.
P 1 row.
Next Row K0 [0:1], *k2tog; rep from * to end.
Cut yarn and draw through rem 6 [7:8] sts. Pull up
tight and fasten off.

knit your left mitten...
Work as given for right mitten to **.

Shape thumb gusset
Next Row K13 [14:15], M1, k2, M1, k15 [16:17].
32 [34:36] sts.
Work 3 rows in st st.
Next Row K13 [14:15], M1, k4, M1, k15 [16:17].
34 [36:38] sts.
Work 3 rows in st st.
Next Row K13 [14:15], M1, k6, M1, k15 [16:17].
36 [38:40] sts.
Work 3 rows in st st.
Next Row K13 [14:15], M1, k8, M1, k15 [16:17].
38 [40:42] sts.
Work 3 rows in st st.
Next Row K13 [14:15], M1, k10, M1, k15 [16:17].
40 [42:44] sts.
Purl 1 row.

Thumb
Next Row K25 [26:27] and turn.
Next Row Cast on 2 sts (using cable cast-on), p14
(including 2 sts just cast on), turn and cast on 2
sts.
Complete as given for thumb of right mitten from
***.
With RS of work facing and using size 9 (5.5mm)
needles, pick up and knit 2 sts across base of
thumb, k across 15 [16:17] unworked sts on left-
hand needle. 30 [32:34] sts.
Work as given for right mitten from ****.

to finish...
Sew in all ends. Join side seams. Full the mittens
following instructions on page 115.

*The deep colours of the yarn
and the dense fabric created
by fulling the mittens provide
the perfect backdrop to show
off the pretty sparkle of the
sequinned butterfly.*

funky fur mittens

MEASUREMENTS

To fit sizes S [M:L]; width around palm is 7
[7½:8]in (18 [19:20.5]cm) and 7 [7½:8]in (18
[19:20.5]cm) long from wrist

GATHER TOGETHER...

materials

A 1 x 1¾oz (50g) ball of medium-weight (aran)
eyelash ribbon yarn (102yd/93m per ball) in
bright pink

B 1 x 1¾oz (50g) ball of light-weight (DK) alpaca
yarn (131yd/120m per ball) in fuschia pink

needles

1 pair of size 10½ (7mm) needles

GAUGE

11 sts and 12 rows to 4in (10cm) measured over
st st (1 row k, 1 row p) using size 10½ (7mm)
needles and 1 strand of A and 2 strands of
B together.

knit note *Wind off half the ball of alpaca. One
strand of A and 2 strands of B are used together
to make a thicker yarn. Make sure that you work
through all three yarns for each stitch.*

*When you use eyelash or faux-fur effect yarns,
you will notice that the back of the work is more
textured than the front. Have a look at the fabric
that you produce and decide whether you want to
show the right or wrong side. Sew the thumb seam
with RS together if you decide to use the WS.*

Wow! These hot pink mittens will warm up even the coldest days. There is no
rib cuff because many fashion yarns are not very elastic and any rib would
soon sag after it had been worn and stretched a few times. A length of cord
with two flamboyant tassels can easily be tightened so you don't lose your
mittens, and is an unusual way to secure them.

Knit your right mitten...

Using size 10½ (7mm) needles, cast on 20
[22:24] sts loosely.
Work 8 rows in st st (1 row k, 1 row p), starting with
a k row.**

Shape thumb gusset

Next Row K10 [11:12], M1, k2, M1, k8 [9:10]. 22
[24:26] sts.
Work 3 rows in st st.
Next Row K10 [11:12], M1, k4, M1, k8 [9:10]. 24
[26:28] sts.
Work 3 rows in st st.
Next Row K10 [11:12], M1, k6, M1, k8 [9:10]. 26
[28:30] sts.
Purl 1 row.

Thumb

Next Row K18 [19:20] and turn.
Next Row Cast on 2 sts (using cable cast-on), p10
(including 2 sts just cast on), turn and cast on
2 sts.
***Work 2½ [2¾:3]in (6 [7:7.5]cm) on these
12 sts only for thumb, ending with a p row.
Measure the knitting next to your thumb, placing
the cast-on sts at the base of your thumb. You may

need to add or subtract rows here to fit your
thumb length.
Next Row K1, (k2tog, k1) 3 times, k2. 9 sts.
P 1 row.
Next Row K1, (k2tog) 4 times.
Cut yarn and thread through rem 5 sts. Pull up tight
and fasten off. Join thumb seam.
With RS of work facing and using size 10½ (7mm)
needles, pick up and knit 2 sts across base of
thumb, k across 8 [9:10] unworked sts on left-hand
needle. 20 [22:24] sts.
****Cont in st st across all sts until mitten
measures 6 [6½:7]in (15 [16.5:18]cm) from
beg of thumb gusset, ending with a p row.
Try the mitten on; it should be approx 1in (2.5cm)
below the top of your longest finger. You may
need to add or subtract rows here to fit your
hand length.

Shape top

Next Row (K1, ssk, k4 [5:6], k2tog, k1) twice. 16
[18:20] sts.
P 1 row.
Next Row * K1, (k2tog) 3 [4:4] times, k1 [0:1]; rep
from * once more.
Cut yarn and draw through rem 10 [10:12] sts.

YARN FOCUS

These mittens are knitted in an unlikely combination of a pure alpaca yarn
and a fashion eyelash yarn. Usually eyelash yarns are used in lighter scarves
or garments, but I wanted to use them for something warmer. To achieve this,
I combined it with two strands of a gorgeous natural-fibre yarn that gives
warmth and structure to the mittens.

knit your left mitten...

Work as given for right mitten to **.

Shape thumb gusset

Next Row K8 [9:10], M1, k2, M1, k10 [11:12]. 22 [24:26] sts.

Work 3 rows in st st.

Next Row K8 [9:10], M1, k4, M1, k10 [11:12]. 24 [26:28] sts.

Work 3 rows in st st.

Next Row K8 [9:10], M1, k6, M1, k10 [11:12]. 26 [28:30] sts.

Purl 1 row.

Thumb

Next Row K16 [17:18] and turn.

Next Row Cast on 2 sts (using cable cast-on), p10 (including 2 sts just cast on), turn and cast on 2 sts.

Complete as given for Thumb of right mitten from ***.

With RS of work facing and using size 10½ (7mm) needles, pick up and knit 2 sts across base of thumb, k across 10 [11:12] unworked sts on left-hand needle. 20 [22:24] sts.

Work as given for right mitten from ****.

to finish...

Sew in all ends. Press all pieces according to instructions on the ball band. Join side seams.

Cord and tassel (make 2)

Cut four strands of B 45in (114cm) long. Tie them together with a knot at both ends. Hook one end over a doorknob or hook, and holding the other knotted end, stand back so that the strands are taut. Insert a pencil into this end and wind it to twist the strands. Keep the strands taut as you wind, twisting until the cord starts to fold up and twist around itself. Keeping the cord taut, remove the end from the doorknob and bring both knotted ends together. Making sure you keep the cord taut, allow the cord to twist around itself. Fold the cord in half. Insert a crochet hook through both thicknesses of the mitten under the thumb gusset. Catch the fold of the cord with the hook and pull through. Pass the ends through the loop and pull to tighten slightly. To make the tassels, tie new knots in both ends of the cord. Cut the looped end and untie the old knots at the other end. Pull the strands apart and trim the bottom of the tassel neatly.

This fashion yarn has an almost feathery texture, used here in combination with alpaca yarn to create a unique and eye-catching fabric.

autumn leaves hooded poncho

By working this poncho from the neck down, it is very easy to alter its length. You could make it longer for an extra-cosy wrap in winter or shorten it for a simple cover-up in summer. Just knit extra rows and work increases as set; keep trying it on until you reach your ideal length. This poncho is knitted on a circular needle so there are no seams to sew up at the end. There are two sets of increasing stitches, at the centre front and centre back. The increase M1 is used (see page 108). After the main piece has been bound off, the stitches for the neck rib are picked up; the hood is shaped using ssk and k2tog, p2tog and ssp (see pages 110–111).

The main body of this poncho is knitted in the round on circular needles; the hood is knitted back and forth on circulars.

YARN FOCUS

For this project, I wanted a yarn that reflected the fabulous colours of autumn; deep rich tones of red, green and bronze. I used a chunky multi-coloured wool yarn with a twist of cotton, which adds texture to the simple stockinette stitch fabric.

DESIGN SECRETS UNRAVELLED…

Instead of using chunky-weight yarn, why not make up a mix of yarns to the same gauge? Put a light-weight (DK) and a medium-weight (aran) yarn together, mixing textures and colours. Alternatively, mix two fine-weight (4ply) wool yarns with a chenille yarn. A multi-coloured cotton light-weight (DK) could be used with a tweed wool in a complementary shade, or a medium-weight (aran) bouclé used with a cotton tape. Transform the poncho for summer by using cotton mixed with silk in soft shades of mauve or blue. Use a summer fashion yarn with slubs and snarls for a beach cover-up. Take the chill off summer evenings by mixing linen with cotton in natural earthy shades.

autumn leaves hooded poncho

This quick-knit project is a great way to start if you have never used circular needles before. See page 114 for further instructions.

See page 114 for further instructions.

MEASUREMENTS

62in (158cm) circumference at widest point and 19in (49cm) long at centre front

GATHER TOGETHER...
materials

5 x 3½oz (100g) hanks of bulky-weight (chunky) multi-coloured wool yarn wrapped with a cotton twist (130yd/120m per hank) in russet/green/mahogany mix

needles and notions

Size 10 (6mm) 24in (60cm)-long circular needle
Size 10 (6mm) 32in (80cm)-long circular needle
Stitch markers

GAUGE

14 sts and 19 rows to 4in (10cm) measured over st st (1 row k, 1 row p) using size 10 (6mm) circular needle

Special abbreviations
PM   place marker

Knit your poncho...

(Knitted from the neck down)

Using the shorter-size 10 (6mm) circular needle, cast on 98 sts and join into a ring, making sure the cast-on sts are not twisted and place a marker to show the beg of the rnd. (Slip this marker on every rnd.)

Knit 2 rnds.

Inc Rnd K24, M1, PM, k1, M1, k48, M1, PM, k1, M1, k24. 102 sts (markers indicate centre front and centre back; slip these markers on every rnd).

Knit 1 rnd.

Inc Rnd K25, M1, k1, M1, k50, M1, k1, M1, k25. 106 sts.

Knit 1 rnd.

Inc Rnd K26, M1, k1, M1, k52, M1, k1, M1, k26. 110 sts.

Knit 1 rnd.

Inc Rnd K27, M1, k1, M1, k54, M1, k1, M1, k27. 114 sts.

Knit 1 rnd.

Cont to inc 4 sts as set on next and every foll alt rnd (transferring to longer needles when necessary) until work measures 19in (49cm) at centre front, ending with an inc rnd.

Purl 1 rnd.
Knit 1 rnd.
Purl 1 rnd.
Bind off loosely knitwise.

knit your hood...

With RS of work facing, and using the shorter-size 10 (6mm) circular needle and beginning at centre front, pick up and k 98 sts around cast-on edge. Place a marker to show beg of next rnd.

Next Rnd *K1, p1; rep from * to end.

Rep this rnd for 1½in (4cm).

Next Rnd *K1, p1; rep from * to last 2 sts, ssk. 97 sts.

Dec Rnd (K1, p1) twice, (k13, k2tog) 5 times, k14, (p1, k1) twice. 92 sts.

Turn and work in rows back and forwards from now on.

Next Row WS (P1, k1) twice, p to last 4 sts, (k1, p1) twice, turn.

Next Row (K1, p1) twice, k to last 4 sts, (p1, k1) twice, turn.

Work in st st and rib border as set until hood measures 8½in (22cm) from top of rib, ending with a WS row.

Shape top

Dec Row Patt 44 sts, ssk, k2tog, patt to end. 90 sts.
Patt 1 row.
Dec Row Patt 43 sts, ssk, k2tog, patt to end. 88 sts.
Patt 1 row.
Dec Row Patt 42 sts, ssk, k2tog, patt to end. 86 sts.
Patt 1 row.
Dec Row Patt 41 sts, ssk, k2tog, patt to end. 84 sts.
Patt 1 row.
Dec Row Patt 40 sts, ssk, k2tog, patt to end. 82 sts.
Dec Row Patt 39 sts, p2tog, ssp, patt to end. 80 sts.
Dec Row Patt 38 sts, ssk, k2tog, patt to end. 78 sts.
Dec Row Patt 37 sts, p2tog, ssp, patt to end. 76 sts.
Dec Row Patt 30 sts, bind off centre 16 sts, patt to end.
Next Row Patt 30 sts.
Next Row Bind off 10 sts, patt to end.
Next Row Patt 20 sts.
Bind off rem 20 sts.
With WS of work facing, rejoin yarn to rem 30 sts and patt to end.
Patt 1 row.
Next Row Bind off 10 sts, patt to end.
Patt 1 row.
Bind off rem 20 sts.

to finish...

Sew in all ends. Press poncho according to instructions on ball bands. Join top hood seam.

new yarn, new look!

I used a mix of white and silver yarns to create a glamorous wintry fabric for this short version of the poncho. It will cover your shoulders or fit snugly under your coat for extra warmth. Work the poncho to a length of 10in (25cm). Make a twisted cord and thread through the rib at the neck. Add two pompoms made of all three yarns (see page 120).

MATERIALS

A Light-weight (DK) fun-fur effect yarn (100% polyester – 98yd/90m per ball) in white
B Medium-weight (aran) cotton/acrylic/ polyester mix bouclé yarn (136yd/125m per ball) in white
C Light-weight (DK) metallic yarn (80% viscose/20% metallized polyester – 218yd/200m per ball) in silver

DESIGN NOTE
Pompoms are very easy to make; they are great for adding a finishing touch to your knitted accessory. Make them with one yarn or combine two, three or more yarns together for a fabulous textured accent. In mohair, they turn into a ball of fluff, while in silk pompoms become an object of luxury. The key to achieving the perfect pompom is to use plenty of yarn; really fill up the hole in your card pompom maker. Trim it neatly into a ball and attach to the ends of a scarf, on the ends of drawstrings, hats, or add to the centre of a knitted corsage.

AND IT DOESN'T END THERE...
Team this shorter poncho or capelet with your favourite evening dress; knit it in silk to cover bare shoulders. For a different evening look, combine metallic yarns for sparkle and slinkiness. For winter, knit it in tweed wool and wear it over an aran or Fair Isle sweater.

good things come in threes

This three-piece set of scarf, hat and wristwarmers is worked in a unique yarn made up of three contrasting yarns (see Yarn Focus). Knit the whole set for a stylishly coordinated look (see Having it All! on page 52) or make just one item if you prefer. The simple k2, p2 rib pattern means that the scarf is extra thick for added warmth, while the hat and wristwarmers will hug you closely to keep out the winter chills. The scarf is enhanced by a thick fringe; the hat features a flamboyant flower brooch for a touch of glamour and individuality; and the wristwarmers have a knitted thumb for extra warmth.

YARN FOCUS

For this set, I used a mix of yarns with contrasting textures to produce a one-of-a-kind fabric. It is exciting to use contrasting yarns next to each other in stripes or in slip-stitch fabrics, but here I wanted something easy to knit in which the yarns, rather than the technique, took centre stage.

The three yarns I chose were a light-weight (DK) soft wool tweed in lavender with subtle slubs of colour; a crisp, shimmering fine (4ply) metallic yarn in vibrant mauve; and a barely-there super-fine-weight mohair in a soft shade of berry. (For specific yarn details, see pages 125–126.)

DESIGN SECRETS UNRAVELLED...

Mixing yarns can be a great way to use very thin yarns that would otherwise take a while to knit up, such as the mohair used here. Of course, you don't have to use only three yarns. You could substitute two thinner yarns for the light-weight tweed: a fine-weight (4ply) cotton and a super-fine-weight (2ply) Shetland wool, for example. Or you could use just two yarns; try a thicker yarn, such as a medium-weight (aran) handspun yarn with slubs and bumps, and contrast it with a light-weight soft mohair or crisp cotton.

The key is to experiment: try different textures together, adding and taking out yarns as you feel. But always keep in mind that you are aiming for a final mix that knits up to the correct gauge.

on the fringes scarf

MEASUREMENTS

5in (12.5cm) wide by 64in (162cm) long

GATHER TOGETHER...

materials

A 3 x 1¾oz (50g) balls of light-weight (DK) tweed wool yarn (123yd/113m per ball) in lavender

B 3 x ⅞oz (25g) balls of sport-weight (4ply) metallic yarn (104yd/95m per ball) in metallic purple

C 2 x ⅞oz (25g) balls of super-fine-weight (2ply) mohair/silk mix yarn (229yd/210m per 25g ball) in purple berry

needles and notions

1 pair of size 10½ (7mm) needles
Piece of cardboard 9in (23cm) wide
Size H/8 (5mm) crochet hook

GAUGE

8 sts and 17 rows to 4in (10cm) measured over unstretched k2, p2 rib using size 10½ (7mm) needles and yarns A, B and C held together.

knit note Three yarns are used together to make a thicker yarn. Make sure that you work through all three yarns for each stitch.

This simple scarf gets its style impact from the use of combined yarns. Once you have cast on, you need only learn a simple two-row pattern repeat to produce a thick k2, p2 rib. Instructions are given for a fringe; alternatively, you could leave the scarf plain.

Knit your scarf...

Using size 10½ (7mm) needles and yarns A, B and C together, cast on 26 sts loosely.

Row 1 RS K2, *p2, k2; rep from * to end.
Row 2 P2, *k2, p2; rep from * to end.
Cont in rib as set until work measures 64in (162cm) from beg, ending with a WS row.
Bind off loosely.

to finish...

Sew in all ends.

make the fringe...

Using yarns A, B and C together, wrap the yarn loosely around the card. Cut the wrapped strands at the bottom and remove the cardboard. Take two lengths of each of the three yarns and fold in half. Using the crochet hook, pull the strands through the edge of the scarf from front to back by catching the fold with the hook. Pass the ends through the folded loop and pull to tighten the knot. Space each bunch of strands evenly along the edge. For a thinner fringe, put one bunch on each knit rib; for a fuller fringe, put one bunch into each rib.

The fringe shows off the three separate yarns used to create the texture of this funky fabric.

flowered-up hat

MEASUREMENTS
Hat – will stretch to fit up to 22in (54cm)
head circumference
Flower – approx 3½in (9cm) in diameter

GATHER TOGETHER...
materials
A 1 x 1¾oz (50g) ball of light-weight (DK) tweed
wool yarn (123yd/113m per ball) in lavender
B 2 x ⅞oz (25g) balls of sport-weight (4ply)
metallic yarn (104yd/95m per ball)
in metallic purple
C 1 x ⅞oz (25g) ball of super-fine-weight (2ply)
mohair/silk mix yarn (229yd/210m per ball)
in purple berry

needles and notions
1 pair of size 10½ (7mm) needles
1 pair of size 6 (4mm) needles
Brooch pin or safety pin

GAUGE
18 sts and 17 rows to 4in (10cm) measured over
unstretched k2, p2 rib using size 10½ (7mm)
needles and yarns A, B and C held together.

*knit note Three yarns are used together to make a
thicker yarn. Make sure that you work through all
three yarns for each stitch.*

The greater part of this hat is worked in unshaped k2, p2 rib. To achieve a better fit, the crown is shaped by decreases. The decreases used – ssk and k2tog, followed by k3tog and k3tog tbl, and finally p2tog and ssp – are worked so that they don't interrupt the rib pattern too visibly. A full explanation of each decrease appears on page 110. The flower brooch is worked on smaller needles because each yarn is used on its own; one yarn is used for each layer. The petals are shaped using k2tog and ssk, and sl2tog-k1-psso (see page 110).

Knit your hat...
Using size 10½ (7mm) needles and yarns A, B and C together, cast on 82 sts loosely.
Row 1 RS K2, *p2, k2; rep from * to end.
Row 2 P2, *k2, p2; rep from * to end.
Cont in rib as set until work measures 4in (10cm) from beg, ending with a WS row.

Shape crown
Dec Row K1, *ssk, p1, (k2, p2) 3 times, k2, p1, k2tog; rep from * 3 times more, k1. 74 sts.
Next Row P2, *k1, (p2, k2) 3 times, p2, k1, p2; rep from * to end.
Dec Row K1, *ssk, (k2, p2) 3 times, k2, k2tog; rep from * 3 times more, k1. 66 sts.
Next Row P4, *(k2, p2) twice, k2, p6; rep from * to last 14 sts, (k2, p2) twice, k2, p4.
Dec Row K1, *ssk, k1, p2, (k2, p2) twice, k1, k2tog; rep from * 3 times more, k1. 58 sts.
Next Row P3, *(k2, p2) twice, k2, p4; rep from * to last 9 sts, k2, p2, k2, p3.
Dec Row K1, *ssk, (p2, k2) twice, p2, k2tog; rep from * 3 times more, k1. 50 sts.
Next Row P2, *k2, p2; rep from * to end.
Dec Row K1, *k3tog tbl, k2, p2, k2, k3tog; rep from * 3 times more, k1. 34 sts.
Next Row P4, *k2, p6; rep from * to last 6 sts, k2, p4.
Dec Row K1, *k3tog tbl, p2, k3tog; rep from * 3 times more, k1. 18 sts.
Dec Row P1, *p2tog, ssp; rep from * 3 times more, p1. 10 sts.
Cut yarns and thread through remaining sts. Draw up tight and fasten off.

to finish...
Using yarn A, join back seam.

knit your flower...
First layer
Using size 6 (4mm) needles and yarn A, cast on 81 sts.
Row 1 WS (K5, p11) 5 times, k1.
Row 2 P1, (k2tog, k7, ssk, p5) 5 times. 71 sts.
****Row 3** (K5, p9) 5 times, k1.
Row 4 P1, (k2tog, k5, ssk, p5) 5 times. 61 sts.
Row 5 (K5, p7) 5 times, k1.
Row 6 P1, (k2tog, k3, ssk, p5) 5 times. 51 sts.
Row 7 (K5, p5) 5 times, k1.
Row 8 P1, (k2tog, k1, ssk, p5) 5 times. 41 sts.
Row 9 (K5, p3) 5 times, k1.
Row 10 P1, (sl2tog-k1-psso, p5) 5 times. 31 sts.
Row 11 (K2tog, k1, k2tog, p1) 5 times, k1. 21 sts.
Cut yarn and thread through rem sts. Draw up tightly and fasten off. Join seam to close circle.
Second layer
Using size 6 (4mm) needles and two strands of yarn B held together, cast on 71 sts and work as given for first layer from **.
Centre
Using size 6 (4mm) needles and yarn C, cast on 52 sts.
Row 1 *K2, lift first of these 2 sts over second and off the needle; rep from * to end. 26 sts.
Row 2 *P2tog; rep from * to end. 13 sts.
Cut yarn and thread through rem sts. Pull up tightly and fasten off. Twist the frills into a pleasing shape.

to finish...
Place centre into middle of second layer and sew through the layer to join. Place second layer on top of first layer and sew through middle to join. Sew a brooch pin or safety pin onto the back. Pin onto hat.

ribby wristwarmers

MEASUREMENTS

7½in (19cm) long; will stretch to fit
small/medium/large sizes

GATHER TOGETHER...

materials

A 1 x 1¾oz (50g) ball of light-weight (DK) tweed
wool yarn (123yd/113m per 50g ball) in lavender
B 1 x ⅞oz (25g) ball of sport-weight (4ply)
metallic yarn (104yd/95m per 25g ball)
in metallic purple
C 1 x ⅞oz (25g) ball of super-fine-weight (2ply)
mohair/silk mix yarn (229yd/210m per 25g ball)
in purple berry

needles and notions

1 pair of size 10½ (7mm) needles
Stitch holder

GAUGE

18 sts and 17 rows to 4in (10cm) measured over
unstretched k2, p2 rib using size 10½ (7mm)
needles and yarns A, B and C held together.

knit note *Three yarns are used together to make a
thicker yarn. Make sure that you work through all
three yarns for each stitch.*

HAVING IT ALL!

The requirements for each project are listed
individually on pages 50–52. But if you just have
to have the complete set, this is what you need:
A 5 x 1¾oz (50g) balls of light-weight (DK) tweed
wool yarn (100% wool – 123yd/113m per ball)
in lavender
B 5 x ⅞oz (25g) balls of sport-weight (4ply)
metallic yarn (80% viscose/20% polyester –
104yd/95m per ball) in metallic purple
C 2 x ⅞oz (25g) balls of super-fine-weight (2ply)
mohair/silk mix yarn (70% super kid mohair/30%
silk – 229yd/210m per ball) in purple berry

Because they are worked in k2, p2 rib, these wristwarmers will stretch to fit your
hand without any shaping. The stitches for the thumb are left on a stitch holder.
When the main part has been completed, you return to these stitches and work
the thumb. Use the cable cast-on method (see page 103) to add extra stitches.

Knit your wristwarmers...

(make 2 the same)
Using size 10½ (7mm) needles and yarns A, B and
C together, cast on 30 sts loosely.
Row 1 RS K2, *p2, k2; rep from * to end.
Row 2 P2, *k2, p2; rep from * to end.
Cont in rib as set until work measures 6in (15cm)
from beg, ending with a WS row.
Place thumb
Next Row Patt 17 sts, slip last 4 sts worked onto a
stitch holder, patt to end.
Next Row Patt 13 sts, cast on 4 sts, patt to end.
Cont in rib as set until work measures 1½in (4cm)
from thumb opening, ending with a WS row.
Bind off loosely.
Thumb
Cast on 3 sts, with RS of work facing, k1, p2, k1
across 4 sts on stitch holder, cast on 3 sts. 10 sts.
Next Row K2, (p2, k2) twice.
Next Row P2, (k2, p2) twice.
Rep these 2 rows twice more.
Bind off loosely in rib.

to finish...

Using yarn A, join thumb seam. Join seam along
bottom edge of thumb, matching ribs. Join side
seam.

*The chunky fabric
of these cosy
wristwarmers will
keep you warm
through winter.*

new yarn, new look!

Using a different set of yarns gives a totally different feel to the rib pattern pieces. Here, I have used a medium-weight (aran) bright raspberry velour tape, a subtly sheened dark raspberry light-weight (DK) cashmere and merino wool mix, and a super-fine-weight (2ply) mohair in a contrasting lime green. The velour yarn adds a suede-like feel to the fabric, which contrasts with the softness of the cashmere/merino mix. The addition of the lime green creates a bright, funky look.

IN THE MIX

A Light-weight (DK) wool and cashmere mix yarn (55% merino wool/33% microfibre/12% cashmere – 136yd/125m per ball) in dark raspberry

B Medium-weight (aran) velour tape (100% nylon – 63yd/58m per ball) in bright raspberry

C Super-fine-weight (2ply) mohair/silk mix yarn (70% super kid mohair/30% silk – 229yd/210m per ball) in lime green

AND IT DOESN'T END THERE...

Instead of contrasting textures, you could use contrasting colours. How about a palette of white, grey and blue for an icy winter theme, or vibrant pink, lime and orange to create a really funky look?

making waves scarf

You can create truly stunning effects with relatively simple techniques. The wave pattern featured here would be eye-catching if knitted in one plain yarn; the combination of two contrasting and vivid yarns, with different textures, mix together to create something truly unique. The soft waves in this scarf are created by an eight-row stitch pattern using two contrasting yarns. The wave of brightly coloured yarn is worked in garter stitch, while the green background is shaped by p2tog, p3tog (see pages 110–111) and yo (see pages 109). The colour switches are easy to handle; simply carry the yarn not in use up the side of the work.

The vibrant colour contrast and funky zig-zag stitch make this scarf a real eye-catcher.

DESIGN SECRETS UNRAVELLED…

Green and pink are on opposite sides of the colour wheel, which is why they zing against each other so wonderfully. This scarf would look very different, although equally effective, with blue-green waves against a blue background, or rich damson waves on dark red. Work it in cotton for a summer-weight scarf, or silk for a glamorous evening accessory. Think of using contrasting textures; you could work the waves in a metallic or a fluffy yarn, or use a chenille yarn against a tweed wool.

YARN FOCUS

The plain green wool is the perfect background to show off the more flamboyant ribbon and mohair-mix yarn. I found that it was easier to work the pattern rows in the plain yarn. The fancy yarn is worked in a simple garter stitch; it needs nothing else.

making waves scarf

MEASUREMENTS

42in (106cm) long by 5½in (14cm) wide

GATHER TOGETHER...

materials

A 1 x 1¾oz (50g) balls of light-weight (DK) wool yarn (131yd/120m per ball) in bright green

B 1 x 1¾oz (50g) balls of light-weight (DK) multi-coloured thin ribbon wrapped with a multi-coloured mohair yarn (154yd/140m per ball) in pink/yellow mix

needles

1 pair of size 7 (4.5mm) needles

GAUGE

28 sts and 24 rows to 4in (10cm) measured over wave st patt using size 7 (4.5mm) needles

---

knit note Carry the yarn that is not in use up the side of the work rather than breaking the yarn and rejoining it for each colour change. This technique is explained further on page 107.

This scarf is made in relatively light-weight materials; the idea was to create a scarf that was more of a colourful accent than a practical and cosy item. If you like the wave pattern but also want to keep warm, simply make the scarf longer and in heavier yarns.

Knit your scarf...

Using size 7 (4.5mm) needles and B, cast on 39 sts.

Knit 3 rows.

Commence wave stitch patt.

Row 1 RS Using A, k to end.

Row 2 Using A, p1, (p2tog) twice, *p2, yo, (p1, yo, p1) into next st, yo, p2, p2tog, p3tog, p2tog; rep from * once more, p2, yo, (p1, yo, p1) into next st, yo, p2, (p2tog) twice, p1.

Row 3 Using A, k to end, working into back of yos of previous row.

Row 4 Using A, as row 2.

Row 5 Using B, k to end, working into back of yos of previous row.

Rows 6, 7 and 8 Using B, knit to end.

These 8 rows form the wave stitch pattern and are repeated.

Cont in patt until scarf measures 42in (106cm), ending with row 8 of patt.

Using B, bind off loosely.

to finish...

Sew in all ends. Press according to instructions on ball bands.

This scarf is perfect for when you want to add a dash of dramatic colour to an outfit.

new yarn, new look!

To make a wider scarf or wrap, work more repeats of the wave stitch pattern. Cast on a multiple of 12 sts plus 3 extra. For this wrap, I contrasted a light-weight (DK) rich purple tweed with a fantastic light-weight (DK) cord in shades of green. Use bulky yarn and larger needles for a really thick wrap, working in one colour for texture. Alternatively, how about using many more than two colours, alternating stripes for a colourful scarf or wrap?

IN THE MIX

A Light-weight (DK) tweed wool yarn (100% wool – 123yd/113m per ball) in dark purple
B Light-weight (DK) nylon-covered linen cord (152yd/140m per ball) in green mix

DESIGN NOTE

The wave pattern is worked over a multiple of 12 sts plus 3 extra for the edge stitches; cast on 51 sts for a wider scarf, 75 sts or more for a wrap. Many traditional stitch patterns use increases and decreases to pull the knitted fabric into waves. By adding more stitches between the shaping stitches, a flatter wave would be made; by arranging them close together, like here, a sharper wave is produced. The decreases pull the fabric down into troughs while the increases (yos) form the peaks of the waves.

AND IT DOESN'T END THERE...

I love combining two thicknesses of yarn together to see what happens; here, the thick tweed yarn has formed a solid wave on a lace base – or is it lace waves on a tweed fabric? This wrap would also look great worked in a metallic yarn with mohair for a hazy evening sparkle. Alternatively, for summer, mix lots of cottons, linens, and fashion yarns in bright colours for a funky beach wrap.

smart girl gloves

Traditionally, gloves are worked in the round using four double-pointed needles, but this project is worked on two needles. This means that there are more seams to sew up at the end, but if you aren't confident using four needles then why miss out on the satisfaction of knitting gloves? It is amazing how the fingers appear out of the stitches for the hand and how the thumb is accommodated into its own space. The process of knitting gloves is explained further on page 113.

The ribbed cuff is worked in a different colour and a different yarn from the main part of the glove; the contrast looks smart and chic.

DESIGN SECRETS UNRAVELLED…

Choosing yarns and colours that you wouldn't ordinarily use can bring unexpected and rewarding results. If you choose a natural shade, why not contrast it with a rib of rich colour such as a deep purple or burgundy? Alternatively, pick a smart colour in an unexpected texture such as chenille or bouclé. Instead of using buttons in complementary shades, add beads, sequins or rhinestones. The addition of pearls would turn these elegantly understated gloves into something truly fabulous.

YARN FOCUS

I wanted a contrast to many of the projects in this book; a calm oasis of natural shades in a vibrant world of colour. Natural shades such as browns, beiges and greys are what I call 'smart' colours – they don't shout at you, they don't demand attention; they just know that they are always in fashion. These colours are always the basics of a smart girl's wardrobe; sophisticated, elegant and stylish. I chose a luxury tweed yarn in a wool and alpaca mix in an oatmeal shade and complemented it with a light-weight (DK) yarn in soft camel.

smart girl gloves

MEASUREMENTS

To fit sizes S [M:L]; width around palm is 7
[8:8¾]in (18 [20.5:22]cm) and 7 [7½:8]in
(18 [19:20.5]cm) long from wrist

GATHER TOGETHER...
materials

A 1 x 1¾oz (50g) ball of light-weight (DK) wool/
alpaca mix yarn (197yd/180m per ball)
in oatmeal

B 1 x 1¾oz (50g) ball of light-weight (DK)
wool yarn (107yd/98m per ball) in camel
Approx 36 mixed size buttons in wood,
shell and natural shades

needles

1 pair of size 3 (3.25mm) needles
1 pair of size 6 (4mm) needles

GAUGE

22 sts and 28 rows to 4in (10cm) measured
over st st (1 row k, 1 row p) using size 6
(4mm) needles and A

The thumb gusset is increased using M1 (see page 108) and the tops of the
fingers and thumb are shaped using k2tog (see page 110). There are plenty
of hints within the instructions to ensure a perfect fit. The cuffs are worked in
k1, p1 rib in a contrasting colour. The buttons add some quirky extra detail.

Knit your right glove...

Using size 3 (3.25mm) needles and B, cast on
40 [44:48] sts loosely.
Row 1 *K1, p1; rep from * to end.
Rep this row until rib measures 2½in (6cm).
Change to size 6 (4mm) needles and A.
Work 2 rows in st st (1 row k, 1 row p), starting
with a k row.**

Shape thumb gusset

Next Row K20 [22:24], M1, k2, M1, k18 [20:22].
42 [46:50] sts.
Work 3 rows in st st.
Next Row K20 [22:24], M1, k4, M1, k18 [20:22].
44 [48:52] sts.
Work 3 rows in st st.
Next Row K20 [22:24], M1, k6, M1, k18 [20:22].
46 [50:54] sts.
Work 3 rows in st st.
Next Row K20 [22:24], M1, k8, M1, k18 [20:22].
48 [52:56] sts.
Work 3 rows in st st.
Next Row K20 [22:24], M1, k10, M1, k18 [20:22].
50 [54:58] sts.
Purl 1 row.

Thumb

Next Row K32 [34:36] and turn.
Next Row Cast on 2 sts (using cable cast-on – see
page 103), p14 (including 2 sts just cast on), turn
and cast on 2 sts.
***Work 2½ [2¾:3]in (6 [7:7.5]cm) on these
16 sts only for thumb, ending with a p row.
Measure the knitting next to your thumb, placing
cast-on sts at base of your thumb. You may

need to add or subtract rows here to fit your
thumb length.
Next Row K1, (k2tog, k1) 5 times. 11 sts.
P 1 row.
Next Row K1, (k2tog) 5 times.
Cut yarn and thread through rem 6 sts. Pull up tight
and fasten off. Join thumb seam.
With RS of work facing, using size 6 (4mm)
needles and A, pick up and k 2 sts across base of
thumb, k across 18 [20:22] unworked sts on left-
hand needle. 40 [44:48] sts.
****Cont in st st without shaping until work
measures 1½ [1¾:2]in (4 [4.5:5]cm) from pick up
sts at base of thumb, ending with a p row. Try the
glove on; it should reach base of your fingers. You
may need to add or subtract rows here to fit your
hand length.

After working the st st for each finger, try the glove
on and measure the knitting against your fingers.
Adjust the length as required.
First finger
Next Row K25 [27:30] sts and turn.
Next Row Cast on 2 sts, p12 [12:14] (including 2
sts just cast on), turn and cast on 2 sts.
Work 2½in (6cm) on these 14 [14:16] sts only for
first finger, ending with a p row.
Next Row K1, (k2tog, k1) 4 [4:5] times, k1 [1:0].
10 [10:11] sts.
P 1 row.
Next Row K1, (k2tog) 4 [4:5] times, k1 [1:0].
Cut yarn and thread through rem 6 sts. Pull up tight
and fasten off. Join finger seam.

Second finger

With RS of work facing, using size 6 (4mm) needles and A, pick up and k 2 sts across base of first finger, k5 [6:6] sts and turn.

Next Row Cast on 1 st, p13 [15:15] (including st just cast on), turn and cast on 1 st.

Work 2¾in (7cm) on these 14 [16:16] sts only for second finger, ending with a p row.

Next Row K1, (k2tog, k1) 4 [5:5] times, k1 [0:0]. 10 [11:11] sts.

P 1 row.

Next Row K1, (k2tog) 4 [5:5] times, k1 [0:0]. Cut yarn and thread through rem 6 sts. Pull up tight and fasten off. Join finger seam.

Third finger

With RS of work facing, using size 6 (4mm) needles and A, pick up and k 2 sts across base of second finger, k5 [6:6] sts and turn.

Next Row Cast on 1 st, p13 [15:15] (including st just cast on), turn and cast on 1 st.

Work 2½in (6cm) on these 14 [16:16] sts only for third finger, ending with a p row.

Next Row K1, (k2tog, k1) 4 [5:5] times, k1 [0:0]. 10 [11:11] sts.

P 1 row.

Next Row K1, (k2tog) 4 [5:5] times, k1 [0:0]. Cut yarn and thread through rem 6 sts. Pull up tight and fasten off. Join finger seam.

Fourth finger

With RS of work facing, using size 6 (4mm) needles and A, pick up and k 4 sts across base of third finger, k across 5 [5:6] unworked sts to end.

Next Row P across all 14 [14:16] rem sts.

Work 2in (5cm) on these 14 [14:16] sts only for fourth finger, ending with a p row.

Next Row K1, (k2tog, k1) 4 [4:5] times, k1 [1:0]. 10 [10:11] sts.

P 1 row.

Next Row K1, (k2tog) 4 [4:5] times, k1 [1:0]. Cut yarn and thread through rem 6 sts. Pull up tight and fasten off.

knit your left glove...

Work as given for Right Glove to **.

Shape thumb gusset

Next Row K18 [20:22], M1, k2, M1, k20 [22:24]. 42 [46:50] sts.

Work 3 rows in st st.

Next Row K18 [20:22], M1, k4, M1, k20 [22:24]. 44 [48:52] sts.

Work 3 rows in st st.

Next Row K18 [20:22], M1, k6, M1, k20 [22:24]. 46 [50:54]sts.

Work 3 rows in st st.

Next Row K18 [20:22], M1, k8, M1, k20 [22:24]. 48 [52:56] sts.

Work 3 rows in st st.

Next Row K18 [20:22], M1, k10, M1, k20 [22:24]. 50 [54:58] sts.

Purl 1 row.

Thumb

Next Row K30 [32:34] and turn.

Next Row Cast on 2 sts, p14 (including 2 sts just cast on), turn and cast on 2 sts.

Complete as given for Thumb of Right Glove from ***

With RS of work facing, using size 6 (4mm) needles and A, pick up and k 2 sts across base of thumb, k across 20 [22:24] unworked sts on left-hand needle. 40 [44:48] sts.

Work as given for Right Glove from ****.

to finish...

Sew in all ends. Press pieces according to instructions on ball band. Sew 18 buttons onto the back of each glove using the photograph for reference. Join side seams.

bramble stitch lacy shawl

Lace stitches look impressively complex, but can be relatively simple to achieve. This lacy shawl is not knitted in a traditional lace stitch, however. The stitch is bramble stitch (sometimes known as trinity stitch), which is usually worked on aran sweaters to form a thick textural fabric. Here, it is transformed into a delicate airy fabric by being worked in a thin yarn on large needles. The clusters of stitches are formed by making three stitches out of one (k1, p1, k1 into the same stitch). On the next pattern row, these three stitches are worked together with k3tog (see page 111).

Bramble stitch is a simple lace stitch that creates a beautiful cobwebby fabric for this shawl.

YARN FOCUS

I wanted a shawl that was soft and light and yet so cosy that you would want to wrap yourself up in its depths. This is a light-weight (DK) mohair yarn in a rich purple. The yarn has quite a short hair so it doesn't fill the spaces too much but still has a luxurious feel. Normally knitted on size 6 (4mm) needles, the yarn becomes as light and airy as a spider's web when knitted on size 13 (9mm) needles.

DESIGN SECRETS UNRAVELLED...

Instead of mohair, you could use a light-weight (DK) silk yarn to create an elegant, draping fabric. Alternatively, you could use a crisp cotton/silk mix for summer evenings, or work the shawl in a traditional Shetland wool yarn for a modern twist on an old tradition. How about a scattering of beads over the shawl? Knit in bright metallic ones on wool or ethnic wooden beads on linen (see page 119), working them randomly on the knit rows. Make up some tassels (see page 120) using a mix of contrasting yarns and sew around the edge. A long exaggerated fringe would add movement when the shawl is worn; you could thread some beads on here and there (thread them onto the fringe and secure with a knot).

bramble stitch lacy shawl

MEASUREMENTS

Approx 70in (178cm) wide by
35in (89cm) long at centre after pressing

GATHER TOGETHER...

materials

4 x ⅞oz (25g) balls of light-weight (DK) mohair
yarn (150yd/138m per ball) in dark purple

needles

1 pair of size 13 (9mm) needles

GAUGE

16 sts and 16 rows to 4in (10cm)
measured over bramble st (see right)
using size 13 (9mm) needles

The shawl is a triangle; you start at the point at the centre of the lower edge and increase out by using a yarnover (yo) at the beginning of each row (see page 109). We've suggested a length here, but you could simply add or subtract rows if you prefer a longer or shorter garment.

Knit your bramble stitch gauge square...

Using size 13 (9mm) needles, cast on 26 sts.
Row 1 K to end.
Row 2 K1, *k3tog, (k1, p1, k1) all into next st;
rep from * to last st, k1.
Row 3 K to end.
Row 4 K1, *(k1, p1, k1) all into next st, k3tog;
rep from * to last st, k1.
Rep these 4 rows until gauge square measures
6in (15cm), ending with a k row.
Bind off loosely.

knit your shawl...

Using size 13 (9mm) needles, cast on 3 sts.
Row 1 Yo, k3. 4sts.
Row 2 K2, (k1, p1, k1) all into next st, k1. 6sts.
Row 3 Yo, k to end. 7sts.
Row 4 Yo, k1, (k1, p1, k1) all into next st, k3tog, (k1, p1, k1) all into next st, k1. 10sts.
Row 5 As row 3.
Row 6 Yo, k1, (k1, p1, k1) all into next st, *k3tog, (k1, p1, k1) all into next st; rep from * to last st, k1.
Row 7 As row 3. 11sts.
Rep rows 6 and 7 until work measures 35in (89cm) from beg, ending with row 6.
(The stitch total will increase by 3 sts on every even-numbered row and by 1 st on every odd-numbered row.)
Bind off loosely.

to finish...

Sew in all ends. Using pins, stretch the shawl out so it measures 70in (178cm) wide along bound-off edge and 35in (89cm) long at centre. Pin the sides out straight so the shawl is a right-angle triangle. Gently steam into shape. Allow to dry and remove the pins.

new yarn, new look!

The bramble stitch looks completely different when worked in a thinner yarn on finer needles. Here, I used a fine-weight (4ply) cotton and size 3 (3.25mm) needles to make a highly textured fabric. Use it to make a neckerchief, in a dusty pastel cotton for summer, or make it in rich-coloured wool for winter. Work as given for the shawl until the neckerchief measures 9in (23cm) long. You could also make one for winter in 100% wool. I chose a bright multi-coloured yarn to work the winter version; the different coloured stripes will get thinner as you work more stitches into the neckerchief. Use size 13 (9mm) needles for an open fabric that is light but will still keep you warm.

IN THE MIX
Summer (top): Fine-weight (4ply) cotton yarn (100% cotton – 186yd/170m per ball) in pale blue

Winter (below): Bulky-weight (chunky) wool multi-coloured yarn (109yd/100m per ball) in yellow/green/pink mix

DESIGN NOTE
Try fulling your neckerchief as I have for the winter version; the clusters form soft blips in a lace fabric. Knit a test sample first to see how much the fabric will shrink.

in a twist
wristwarmers

Wristwarmers are a great way to keep your hands warm while still being able to use your fingers – for knitting, of course! These are worked in a k2, p2 rib for a snug fit and feature a simple cable panel on the back of each hand. The panel is worked using C4F and C4B to twist the cables and Cr3L and Cr3R to move the ropes across the fabric. The thumb gusset is increased out of the hand by M1 (see page 108). See page 112 for further instructions on cables.

Cables are fun to make (they're easier than they look) and show up crisply when worked in this smooth yarn.

DESIGN SECRETS UNRAVELLED…

Go for easy colour with a multi-coloured wool yarn or use up your stash of medium-weight (aran) yarns by working the wristwarmers in stripes to create a funky look. You could mix up a yarn of two light-weight (DK) yarns, such as wool mixed with alpaca, or metallic mixed with a tweed. The tight cable would look more relaxed if knitted in a handspun yarn with slubs and bumps.

YARN FOCUS

These wristwarmers are practical items that are made special by using a luxury yarn. I used a wool and cashmere mix medium-weight (aran) yarn for softness and warmth. The cashmere lightens the wool. I didn't want a thick fabric, and this yarn is so light you will hardly know you're wearing it. The rich purple is understated but shows off the cable details beautifully.

MEASUREMENTS

6½in (16.5cm) circumference (unstretched)
by 6½in (16.5cm) long.
Will stretch to fit palm circumference
of up to 9in (23cm)

GATHER TOGETHER...

materials

2 x 1¾oz (50g) balls of medium-weight (aran)
wool/cashmere mix yarn (98yd/90m per ball)
in dark purple

needles

1 pair of size 6 (4mm) needles
cable needle

GAUGE

36 sts and 27 rows to 4in (10cm) measured over
unstretched k2, p2 rib using size 6 (4mm) needles

SPECIAL ABBREVIATIONS

C4F	slip next 2 sts onto a cable needle at front of work, k2, k2 from cable needle
C4B	slip next 2 sts onto a cable needle at back of work, k2, k2 from cable needle
Cr3L	slip next 2 sts onto a cable needle at front of work, p1, k2 from cable needle
Cr3R	slip next st onto a cable needle at back of work, k2, p1 from cable needle

Knitting the cable panel

Throughout the project pattern you will refer back to these instructions for knitting the cable panel:

CABLE PANEL (12 STS)
Row 1 K2, p2, C4F, p2, k2.
Row 2 P2, k2, p4, k2, p2.
Row 3 K2, p2, k4, p2, k2.
Row 4 As row 2.
Row 5 As row 1.
Row 6 As row 2.
Row 7 (Cr3L, Cr3R) twice.
Row 8 K1, p4, k2, p4, k1.
Row 9 P1, C4B, p2, C4B, p1.
Row 10 As row 8.
Row 11 (Cr3R, Cr3L) twice.
Row 12 P2, k2, p4, k2, p2.

These practical and stylish wristwarmers are made special by the cable-panel detail. Cables look complicated but are actually quite simple, and also fun to do. See below left for the cable panel pattern.

knit your right wristwarmer...

Using size 6 (4mm) needles, cast on 52 sts loosely.
Foundation Row 1 (K2, p2) 3 times, k4, (P2, k2) 9 times.
Foundation Row 2 (P2, k2) 9 times, p4, (k2, p2) 3 times.
Commence cable panel.
Row 1 RS (K2, p2) twice, work row 1 of cable panel, (p2, k2) 8 times.
Row 2 (P2, k2) 8 times, work row 2 of cable panel, (k2, p2) twice.
Row 3 (K2, p2) twice, work row 3 of cable panel, (p2, k2) 8 times.
Row 4 (P2, k2) 8 times, work row 4 of cable panel, (k2, p2) twice.
These 4 rows form rib and set cable panel.
Beg with row 5 of cable panel, patt 22 more rows, ending with row 10 of cable panel.

Shape thumb gusset

Keeping cable panel correct
Next Row Patt 26 sts, M1, k2, M1, patt to end. 54 sts.
Next Row Patt 24 sts, p4, patt to end.
Next Row Patt 26 sts, k1, M1, k2, M1, k1, patt to end. 56 sts.
Next Row Patt 24 sts, p6, patt to end.
Next Row Patt 26 sts, k1, M1, k4, M1, k1, patt to end. 58 sts.
Next Row Patt 24 sts, p8, patt to end.
Next Row Patt 26 sts, k1, M1, k6, M1, k1, patt to end. 60 sts.
Next Row Patt 24 sts, p10, patt to end.
Next Row Patt 26 sts, k1, M1, k8, M1, k1, patt to end. 62 sts.
Next Row Patt 24 sts, p12, patt to end.

Thumb

Next Row Patt 26 sts, k12 and turn.
Next Row Cast on 2 sts (using cable cast-on – see page 103), p14 (including 2 sts just cast on), turn and cast on 2 sts.
Work 7 rows in st st (1 row k, 1 row p) on these 16 sts only for thumb.
Knit 1 row.
Bind off loosely.
Join thumb seam.
With RS of work facing and using size 6 (4mm) needles, pick up and k 2 sts across base of thumb, patt across 24 unworked sts on left-hand needle. 52 sts.
Cont in patt until work measures approx 6½in (16.5cm), ending with row 6 of cable panel.
Bind off in patt.

knit your left wristwarmer...

Using size 6 (4mm) needles, cast on 52 sts loosely.
Foundation Row 1 (K2, p2) 9 times, k4, (P2, k2) 3 times.
Foundation Row 2 (P2, k2) 3 times, p4, (k2, p2) 9 times.
Commence cable panel.
Row 1 RS (K2, p2) 8 times, work row 1 of cable panel, (p2, k2) twice.
Row 2 (P2, k2) twice, work row 2 of cable panel, (k2, p2) 8 times.

Row 3 (K2, p2) 8 times, work row 3 of cable panel, (p2, k2) twice.

Row 4 (P2, k2) twice, work row 4 of cable panel, (k2, p2) 8 times.

These 4 rows form rib and set cable panel.
Beg with row 5 of cable panel, patt 22 more rows, ending with row 10 of cable panel.

Shape thumb gusset

Keeping cable panel correct
Next Row Patt 24 sts, M1, k2, M1, patt to end. 54 sts.

Next Row Patt 26 sts, p4, patt to end.
Next Row Patt 24 sts, k1, M1, k2, M1, k1, patt to end. 56 sts.

Next Row Patt 26 sts, p6, patt to end.
Next Row Patt 24 sts, k1, M1, k4, M1, k1, patt to end. 58 sts.

Next Row Patt 26 sts, p8, patt to end.
Next Row Patt 24 sts, k1, M1, k6, M1, k1, patt to end. 60 sts.

Next Row Patt 26 sts, p10, patt to end.
Next Row Patt 24 sts, k1, M1, k8, M1, k1, patt to end. 62 sts.

Next Row Patt 26 sts, p12, patt to end.

Thumb

Next Row Patt 24 sts, k12 and turn.
Next Row Cast on 2 sts (using cable cast-on), p14 (including 2 sts just cast on), turn and cast on 2 sts.
Work 8 rows in st st (1 row k, 1 row p) on these 16 sts only for thumb.
Knit 1 row.
Bind off loosely.
Join thumb seam.
With RS of work facing and using size 6 (4mm) needles, pick up and k 2 sts across base of thumb, patt across 26 unworked sts on left-hand needle. 52 sts.
Cont in patt until work measures approx 6½in (16.5cm), ending with row 6 of cable panel.
Bind off in patt.

to finish...

Sew in all ends. Join side seams.

This is a fabulous single-ply handspun yarn in a range of colours – greens, browns, russets, pale pinks and maroons. The yarn has thick and thin sections so the stitches are uneven. This version of the wristwarmers appears more organic and not as structured as the other pair. I have shown them here without knitted thumbs, making them easier and quicker to knit, and worn over a pair of gloves for extra warmth.

IN THE MIX
Medium-weight (aran) handspun multi-coloured wool yarn (100% wool – 137yd/126m per ball) in cream, green and brown

shake your pompoms ski hat

This ski hat complete with earflaps is warm, practical and just a bit flirty in hot pink and metallic thread. The k2, p2 rib means that the hat fits snugly, while a thin stripe of metallic adds a highlight to stockinette stitch. The crown is shaped using k2tog (see page 110). The earflaps are picked up from the rib and then shaped using k2tog and ssk (see page 110). The ties are small plaits made from both yarns, and the whole hat is topped off with a cute pompom (see page 120 for instructions on making the pompom).

Simple shaping creates the earflaps that will help to keep you stylishly warm through the coldest of winters.

YARN FOCUS

Tweed yarns are available in a wide range of colours apart from the traditional rich country shades. I wanted a thick, warm fabric for this hat, and this medium-weight (aran) tweed wool was perfect. To give the hat a modern twist, I chose a fabulous pink and striped it through with a complementary shade of metallic mauve. The contrast between the two is striking but works extremely well, and is highlighted by the jaunty pompom.

DESIGN SECRETS UNRAVELLED...

The thin stripe adds sparkle and interest to a piece of stockinette stitch. You could work the stripe in a textured yarn such as a bouclé or chenille rather than using a contrasting colour. Use two strands of a thinner yarn such as a fine-weight (4ply) mohair or shiny viscose yarn to make up a medium-weight (aran) yarn for the stripe. But if your main yarn looks fabulous on its own, omit the stripe. Mix a medium-weight (aran) yarn from two light-weight (DK) wools, or one wool yarn with one mohair. Alternatively, you could use a multi-coloured yarn with splashes of colour in dark shades of bronzes, golds and reds, or use all white yarns for a soft, snowy creation.

shake your pompoms ski hat

MEASUREMENTS
To fit head circumference 20 [22]in (51 [56]cm)

GATHER TOGETHER...
materials
A 1 x 3½oz (100g) ball of medium-weight (aran) tweed wool yarn (186yd/170m per ball) in brilliant pink
B 1 x 7/8oz (25g) ball of fine-weight (4ply) metallic yarn (104yd/95m per ball) in metallic mauve

needles
1 pair of size 7 (4.5mm) needles
1 pair of size 8 (5mm) needles

GAUGE
16 sts and 23 rows to 4in (10cm) measured over st st using size 8 (5mm) needles and A

knit note *Two strands of the metallic yarn (B) are used together to make a thicker yarn. Make sure that you work through both strands for each stitch.*

The earflaps and pompom on this hat make it fun and flirty. For a more simply chic look, make the hat on its own without the embellishments.

Knit your hat...
Using size 7 (4.5mm) needles and A, cast on 82 [90] sts loosely.
Row 1 RS K2, *p2, k2; rep from * to end.
Row 2 P2, *k2, p2; rep from * to end.

1st size only
Rep these 2 rows 3 times more, dec 1 st at end of last row. 81 sts.

2nd size only
Rep these 2 rows 3 times more, inc 1 st at end of last row. 91 sts.

Both sizes
Change to size 8 (5mm) needles and work 2 rows in st st (1 row k, 1 row p) starting with a k row. Working in a stripe pattern of 2 rows B, 6 rows A, work a further 22 rows in st st.

Shape crown
Keeping stripe patt correct:
2nd size only
Dec Row K1, (k2tog, k7) 10 times. 81 sts.
Work 3 rows.

Both sizes
Dec Row K1, (k2tog, k6) 10 times. 71 sts.
Work 3 rows.
Dec Row K1, (k2tog, k5) 10 times. 61 sts.
Work 1 row.
Dec Row K1, (k2tog, k4) 10 times. 51 sts.
Work 1 row.
Dec Row K1, (k2tog, k3) 10 times. 41 sts.
Work 1 row.
Dec Row K1, (k2tog, k2) 10 times. 31 sts.
Work 1 row.
Dec Row K1, (k2tog, k1) 10 times. 21 sts.
Work 1 row.
Dec Row K1, (k2tog) 10 times. 11 sts.

Cut yarn and thread through rem sts. Pull up tight and fasten off.

Right earflap
With RS of work facing, using size 8 (5mm) needles and A, and beginning in the 9th [13th] st from side edge, pick up and knit 20 sts along cast-on edge.
Next Row WS K2, p16, k2.
Next Row K to end.
Rep these rows 4 times more then WS row again.
Dec Row K2, ssk, k to last 4 sts, k2tog, k2. 18sts.
Next Row K2, p to last 2 sts, p2.
Cont to dec 2 sts as set on next and every foll RS row to 6 sts.
Knit 2 rows.
Bind off.

Left earflap
With RS of work facing, using size 8 (5mm) needles and A, and beginning in the 27th st from last st of right earflap, pick up and knit 20 sts along cast-on edge.
Complete as given for Right Earflap.

to finish...
Sew in all ends. Press according to instructions on ball bands. Join back seam.
Ties (make 2)
Cut two 60in (152cm) lengths of A and two 60in (152cm) lengths of B. Thread a large-eyed needle with all four strands. Use the needle to pull the strands through the bound-off edge of one earflap. Level the ends and divide the strands into two bunches of A (two strands each) and one of B (four strands). Plait the three strands until tie measures 12in (30cm). Tie into a knot to secure and trim the ends into a small tassel (see detail, top).
Pompom
Make a small pompom (see page 120) using both yarns. Stitch into place at centre of crown.

new yarn, new look!

Stripes don't have to be in contrasting colours; you can make an interesting fabric by combining two similar colours in different textures. With the cream hat, I used a medium-weight (aran) tweed and combined it with a mohair yarn in cream. Although the mohair yarn is medium-weight (aran), it needed two strands to make it up to the thickness of the tweed yarn. This makes a fantastic wintry-looking ski hat; warm and thick with subtle texture changes.

You can also work with contrasts of texture. With the lilac hat, I love the contrast of plain wool and a textured yarn; I used two strands of light-weight (DK) yarn for the rib with a pompom in the same pale pink. I made up a yarn mix of bulky-weight (chunky) chenille and fine-weight (4ply) tweed; these make a thick, cosy fabric with the luxury of the plush and velvety chenille and flashes of colour of the tweed.

IN THE MIX

Cream hat

A Medium-weight (aran) tweed wool yarn (80% wool/20% alpaca – 182yd/166m per ball) in light cream with brown and black fleck

B Medium-weight (aran) mohair/wool mix yarn (76% lambswool/26% kid mohair/4% nylon – 153yd/140m per ball) in cream

Lilac hat

A Light-weight (DK) wool (100% wool – 131yd/120m per ball) in pale pink

B Bulky-weight (chunky) chenille yarn (100% cotton – 153yd/140m per ball) in lilac

C Fine-weight (4ply) tweed wool yarn (100% wool – 162yd/90m per ball) in pink and purple mix

beaded
beauties

Usually a scarf is cast on at the bottom and knitted until it is long enough. Here, however, I wanted these scarves to have vertical stripes of texture and colour; this is easily achieved by knitting them sideways. There are a lot of stitches to cast on, so it helps to place stitch markers every fifty stitches to make counting easier. Use a circular needle to accommodate all the stitches. The scarves are worked in stripes of garter stitch, stockinette stitch and seed (UK: moss) stitch. The beads, buttons and sequins are strung onto a separate thread and knitted in (see page 119).

The mixture of stitches adds texture and interest to the vertical stripes in this fresh-looking summery scarf.

DESIGN SECRETS UNRAVELLED…

Make up your own mix from light-weight (DK) and medium-weight (aran) yarns. You could use more than five colours and yarns. Add into the mix a couple of textured yarns such as chenille, bouclé, tweed or metallic. Choose complementary colours such as mauve, pink and cream; add a flash of vibrant colour such as gold to a collection of greens; or add rich purple to shades of blue. Add wooden beads to a scarf knitted in natural shades, or amethyst chips to one knitted in rich purples and plums.

YARN FOCUS

The five yarns that I chose for this scarf were a light-weight (DK) cord in pink and mauve, a medium-weight (aran) velour tape in cream, a medium-weight (aran) bouclé in cream and a light-weight (DK) cotton/viscose yarn in mauve. The velour and bouclé add texture to the fabric, while the viscose yarn adds shine. The stitches worked in the cord yarns sit separately from each other, adding an openness to the fabric.

summer scorcher

MEASUREMENTS
Approx 63in (160cm) long by 4in (10cm) wide

GATHER TOGETHER...
materials
1 x 1¾oz (50g) balls of light-weight (DK) nylon-covered linen cord (152yd/140m per ball) in each of pink and mauve

1 x ⅞oz (25g) balls of medium-weight (aran) velour tape (63yd/58m per ball) in cream

1 x 1¾oz (50g) ball of medium-weight (aran) cotton/acrylic/polyester mix bouclé yarn (136yd/125m per ball) in cream

1 x 1¾oz/50g balls of light-weight (DK) cotton/viscose yarn (119yd/110m per ball) in mauve

1 x small ball of thin crochet cotton in cream for stringing beads onto

Approx 180 assorted shaped and round beads, buttons and sequins in co-ordinating colours

needles
Size 6 (4mm) 32in (80cm)-long circular needle

GAUGE
21 sts and 32 rows to 4in (10cm) measured over st st using size 6 (4mm) circular needle

Special abbreviations
PB place bead

Making the multi-yarn ball
Pull out 9 arm's lengths of the first yarn and wind it into a ball. Tie on the second colour, leaving long ends to weave in during knitting. Pull out 8 arm's lengths and continue winding onto the ball. Join on the third colour and pull out 6 arm's lengths and wind it onto the ball. Continue in this way, changing the colour sequence and the amount of each yarn used each time. Make up a 1¾oz (50g) ball.

The beads add something special to this scarf. Note that the stringing thread is only used on each bead row and is then cut; you need only string 18 beads at any time (see page 119). Use the bead thread and the multi-yarn together on every bead row. Make sure to knit through both strands for each stitch.

Knit your scarf...
Using size 6 (4mm) circular needle, cast on 329 sts. (Work backwards and forwards on needle throughout.)
Knit 3 rows.
Bead Row 1 RS K5, PB, (k13, PB) 5 times, k18, PB, (k27, PB) 5 times, k18, PB, (k13, PB) 5 times, k5.
Knit 3 rows.
**Bead Row 2 K9, PB, (k13, PB) 5 times, k18, PB, (k27, PB) 5 times, k10, PB, (k13, PB) 5 times, k9.
Knit 3 rows.
Bead Row 3 K2, PB, (k13, PB) 5 times, k18, PB, (k27, PB) 5 times, k24, PB, (k13, PB) 5 times, k2. **
Purl 1 row.
Knit 1 row.
Purl 1 row.
Bead Row 4 K7, PB, (k13, PB) 5 times, k18, PB, (k27, PB) 5 times, k14, PB, (k13, PB) 5 times, k7.
Purl 1 row.
Knit 1 row.
Purl 1 row.
Bead Row 5 K11, PB, (k13, PB) 5 times, k18, PB, (k27, PB) 5 times, k6, PB, (k13, PB) 5 times, k11.
Purl 1 row.
Next Row K1, *p1, k1; rep from * to end.
Rep this row once more.
Bead Row 6 Patt 3, PB, (patt 13, PB) 5 times, patt 19, PB, (patt 27, PB) 5 times, patt 21, PB, (patt 13, PB) 5 times, patt 3.
Patt 3 rows.
Bead Row 7 Patt 9, PB, (k13, PB) 5 times, patt 17, PB, (patt 27, PB) 5 times, patt 11, PB, (patt 13, PB) 5 times, patt 9.
Patt 3 rows.
Bead Row 8 Patt 5, PB, (patt 13, PB) 5 times, patt 19, PB, (patt 27, PB) 5 times, patt 17, PB, (patt 13, PB) 5 times, patt 5.

Patt 1 row.
Knit 2 rows.
Work from ** to ** once more.
Knit 2 rows.
Bind off loosely.

to finish...
Sew in all ends. Press carefully; beads sometimes hold heat after being steamed.

winter warmer

MEASUREMENTS
Approx 70in (177cm) long by 3in (7.5cm) wide

GATHER TOGETHER...
materials
1 x 1¾oz/50g balls of light-weight (DK) wool
yarn (131yd/120m per ball) in each of brown and
pumpkin
1 x 1¾oz/50g balls of light-weight (DK) cotton/
silk mix yarn (218yd/200m per ball) in tan
1 x 1¾oz/50g balls of light-weight (DK) wool
tweed yarn (123yd/113m per ball) in red
1 x ⅞oz/25g balls of light-weight (DK) angora/
wool mix multi-coloured yarn (124yd/112m
per ball) in gold/pink/brown mix
1 x small ball of crochet cotton in brown for
stringing beads
Approx 120 assorted shaped and round beads,
buttons and sequins in co-ordinating colours

needles
Size 6 (4mm) 32in (80cm)-long circular needle

GAUGE
19 sts and 32 rows to 4in (10cm) measured over
st st using size 6 (4mm) circular needle

knit note *Make up a multi-yarn ball – see
instructions for Summer Scorcher Scarf.*

DESIGN SECRETS UNRAVELLED...
You can use heavier yarns for this version
of the scarf. Wool, tweed, chenille, wool
bouclé, mohair and angora are all rich-
looking yarns. Try a different colourway;
shades of purples, shades of gold, or
a collection of deep berry colours. Add
sparkle with sequins or drama with fiery
crystals. Use metal buttons instead of shell
and combine these with sequins in shades
of gold and bronze.

Vertical stripes create a pleasing
depth of colour and pattern if worked
in rich autumnal shades and lush
textures for a winter-weight scarf.

Knit your scarf...
Work as given for the Summer Scorcher Scarf until
bead row 6 has been completed.
Patt 2 rows.
Bind off loosely in patt.

to finish...
Sew in all ends. Press carefully; beads sometimes
hold heat after being steamed.

YARN FOCUS
I used warmer shades and yarns for this version:
light-weight (DK) wool in brown and pumpkin
orange; tweed wool in rich red; cotton/silk yarn
in golden tan; and a multi-coloured angora/wool
yarn in shades of gold, pink and brown. The angora
adds lightness to the tweed and wool, while the
cotton/silk mix offers a dry texture compared to
the other yarns.

cashmere chic set

This four-piece set of scarf, beret, gloves and corsage is worked in a luxurious wool and cashmere mix yarn in a deep, rich shade of red. Knit the whole set or pick out individual pieces to make up your own look. The scarf and beret are knitted in seed (UK: moss) stitch using two strands of the yarn, producing a lush, richly textured fabric. The gloves and corsage need more precise shaping so are worked in one strand of yarn. The gloves have a pretty heart motif on the back of each hand, and the petals of the corsage are worked in garter stitch.

DESIGN SECRETS UNRAVELLED…

This set would look equally good worked in a light-weight (DK) pure wool or wool tweed. Choose a yarn that is smooth rather than textured; otherwise, the seed (moss) stitch will not be clearly defined. Try altering the colours too; the scarf edgings could be worked in a contrasting colour to the scarf or in a mohair yarn to make them light as a feather. Work the gloves in a bright colour with the corsage to match. Knit the corsage in a bright cotton yarn and pin it to the beret, worked in a contrasting cotton/ silk mix yarn for warmer days.

YARN FOCUS

For this set, I used a luxury yarn; the wool and cashmere mix is soft, warm and stylish. It is a light-weight (DK) yarn that shows off the texture of the seed (moss) stitch beautifully. The deep rich red adds to the overall look of extravagance.

through the keyhole scarf

MEASUREMENTS
5½in (14cm) wide by 40in (101.5cm) long

GATHER TOGETHER...
materials
3 x 1¾oz (50g) balls of light-weight (DK) wool/
cashmere mix yarn (142yd/130m per ball) in
claret red

needles
1 pair of size 10 (6mm) needles

GAUGE
16 sts and 26 rows to 4in (10cm) measured over
seed (moss) stitch using size 10 (6mm) needles
and two strands of yarn together

*knit note Two yarns are used together to make
a thicker yarn. Make sure that you work through
both yarns for each stitch.*

HAVING IT ALL!
The requirements for each project are listed
individually on pages 80–83. But if you just have
to have the complete set, this is what you need:
7 x 1¾oz (50g) balls of light-weight (DK) wool/
cashmere mix yarn (142yd/130m per ball) in
claret red

The fancy ends of this scarf can be threaded through the keyhole to keep the
scarf snug around your neck even on the windiest of days. It is worked in seed
(moss) stitch using two strands of yarn together, so is very quick to knit. The
large holes in the edgings are made with multiple yarnovers (yos) and then
several stitches are worked into them (see page 109).

Knit your scarf...
Using size 10 (6mm) needles and two strands of
yarn together, cast on 20 sts loosely.
Row 1 RS *K1, p1; rep from * to end.
Row 2 *P1, k1; rep from * to end.
These 2 rows form seed (moss) stitch and are
repeated.
Cont in patt until scarf measures 4in (10cm),
ending with a WS row.
Divide for keyhole:
Next Row Patt 10 sts, join in a new yarn (of two
strands) and use this to patt to end.
Working both sides at the same time, work in patt
until keyhole measures 3in (7.5cm), ending with
a WS row.
Next Row Patt across all 20 sts (joining two sides
into one again).
Cut off second yarn.
Cont in patt until scarf measures 32in (81.5cm),
ending with a WS row.
Bind off loosely in patt.

Edging (make 2)
Using size 10 (6mm) needles and two strands of
yarn together, cast on 13 sts loosely.
Foundation Row 1 K3, p10.
Foundation Row 2 K2, (yo) 4 times, k2tog, k6, turn.
Row 1 P7, (k1, p1) twice into 4-yo loop, p2.
Row 2 K16.
Row 3 K3, p13.
Row 4 K2, (yo) 5 times, k2tog, k9 and turn.
Row 5 P10, (k1, p1, k1, p1, k1) into 5-yo loop, p2.
Row 6 K20.

Row 7 K3, p17.
Row 8 Bind off 7 sts, k2 (including last st used in
bind-off), (yo) 4 times, k2tog, k6 and turn.
These 8 rows form the edging and are repeated.
Cont in patt until edging fits across end of scarf,
ending with row 7 of patt.
Bind off loosely.

to finish...
Sew in all ends. Press according to instructions on
ball band. Sew an edging onto each end of the
scarf.

*The lacy edging on the
scarf provides an attractive
flounce of detail.*

seed stitch beret

Using two strands of yarn together, the stylish beret is worked in seed (moss) stitch. The k1, p1 rib fits snugly around your head. After the rib, you increase stitches using M1 (see page 108), then shape the crown using p3tog and k3tog (see page 111) so that the seed (moss) stitch pattern isn't interrupted.

MEASUREMENTS
To fit head circumference 20 [22]in (51 [56]cm)

GATHER TOGETHER...
materials
2 x 1¾oz (50g) balls of light-weight (DK) wool/cashmere mix yarn (142yd/130m per ball) in claret red

needles
1 pair of size 8 (5mm) needles
1 pair of size 10 (6mm) needles

GAUGE
16 sts and 26 rows to 4in (10cm) measured over seed (moss) stitch using size 10 (6mm) needles and two strands of yarn together

knit note Two yarns are used together to make a thicker yarn. Make sure that you work through both yarns for each stitch.

Knit your beret...
Using size 8 (5mm) needles and two strands of yarn together, cast on 68 [76] sts.
Row 1 *K1, p1; rep from * to end.
This row forms the rib.
Work a further 4 rows in rib.
Inc Row Rib 4 [6], (rib 1 [2], M1, rib 2, M1) 20 [16] times, rib 4 [6]. 108 sts.
Change to size 10 (6mm) needles.
Row 1 RS *K1, p1; rep from * to end.
Row 2 *P1, k1; rep from * to end.
These 2 rows form seed (moss) stitch and are repeated. Work a further 20 rows in patt.

Shape top
Row 23 K1, p1, k1, *p3tog, (k1, p1) 3 times, k3tog, (p1, k1) 3 times; rep from * to last 15 sts, p3tog, (k1, p1) 3 times, k3tog, p1, k1, p1. 84 sts.
Patt 7 rows.

Row 31 K1, p1, *k3tog, (p1, k1) twice, p3tog, (k1, p1) twice; rep from * to last 12 sts, k3tog, (p1, k1) twice, p3tog, k1, p1. 60 sts.
Patt 7 rows.
Row 39 K1, *p3tog, k1, p1, k3tog, p1, k1; rep from * to last 9 sts, p3tog, k1, p1, k3tog, p1. 36 sts.
Patt 3 rows.
Row 43 *K1, p1, k1, p3tog; rep from * to end. 24 sts.
Patt 1 row.
Row 45 *K3tog, p1; rep from * to end. 12 sts.
Purl 1 row.
Cut yarn and thread through rem sts. Pull up tight and fasten off.

to finish...
Sew in all ends. Press according to instructions on ball band. Join back seam.

classy corsage

Each of the six petals is knitted separately; they are then joined at the base to produce a large bloom. The petal is shaped by working three times into one st (see page 109) and decreased using ssk, k2tog and sl2tog-k1-psso (see pages 110–111). The centre is filled with sequins and beads.

MEASUREMENTS
Flower is approx 5in (12.5cm) in diameter

GATHER TOGETHER...
materials
1 x 1¾oz (50g) balls of light-weight (DK) wool/cashmere mix yarn (142yd/130m per ball) in claret red
Sequins and small beads

needles and notions
1 pair of size 3 (3.25mm) needles
Brooch pin or safety pin

GAUGE
24 sts and 48 rows to 4in (10cm) measured over garter stitch (every row k) using size 3 (3.25mm) needles and one strand of yarn

Knit your corsage...
Petal (make 6)
Using size 3 (3.25mm) needles and single strand of yarn, cast on 3 sts and knit 1 row.
Row 1 RS K1, (k into front, back and front) into next st, k1. 5 sts.
Rows 2, 4, 6 Knit.
Row 3 K2, (k into front, back and front) into next st, k2. 7 sts.
Row 5 K3, (k into front, back and front) into next st, k3. 9 sts.
Row 7 K4, (k into front, back and front) into next st, k4. 11 sts.
Knit 5 rows.
Row 13 K1, ssk, k5, k2tog, k1. 9 sts.
Knit 5 rows.
Row 19 K1, ssk, k3, k2tog, k1. 7 sts.
Knit 3 rows.

Row 23 K1, ssk, k1, k2tog, k1. 5 sts.
Knit 3 rows.
Row 27 K1, sl2tog-k1-psso, k1. 3 sts.
Knit 1 row.
Row 29 Sl2tog-k1-psso. 1 st.
Cut yarn and thread through rem st.

to finish...
Sew in all ends. Fold each petal in half (with RS together) at the base and sew the side edges together for ½in (1.5cm). Place the petals side by side and run a gathering thread through each to join. Pull the thread tight and repeat through all petals again to form a circle. Pull the thread tight so the flower becomes dish-shaped. Secure the thread. Fill the centre with sequins and beads, sewing the beads onto the top of the sequins. Sew a brooch pin or safety pin onto the back.

love-heart gloves

MEASUREMENTS

To fit sizes S [M:L]; width around palm is 7 [8:8¾]in (18 [20.5:22]cm) and 7 [7½:8]in (18 [19:20.5]cm) long from wrist

GATHER TOGETHER...
materials

2 [2:2] x 1¾oz (50g) balls of light-weight (DK) wool/cashmere mix yarn (142yd/130m per ball) in claret red

needles

1 pair of size 3 (3.25mm) needles
1 pair of size 6 (4mm) needles
GAUGE

22 sts and 30 rows to 4in (10cm) measured over st st (1 row k, 1 row p) using size 6 (4mm) needles and one strand of yarn

The cute heart-shaped motif is worked on the back of each hand in seed (moss) stitch to stand out well against the stockinette stitch.

To make the gloves fit perfectly, use one strand of yarn throughout and stockinette stitch. There is a k1, p1 rib cuff for a snug fit. The thumb gusset is shaped out from the hand using M1 (see page 108) and the fingers are shaped at the top using k2tog (see page 110). The technique of knitting gloves is explained on page 113.

Heart Motif Panel (13 sts)
Row 1 RS K6, p1, k6.
Row 2 P5, k1, p1, k1, p5.
Row 3 K4, p1, (k1, p1) twice, k4.
Row 4 P3, k1, (p1, k1) 3 times, p3.
Row 5 K2, p1, (k1, p1) 4 times, k2.
Row 6 P1, (k1, p1) 6 times.
Row 7 As row 6.
Row 8 As row 6.
Row 9 As row 6.
Row 10 As row 6.
Row 11 As row 6.
Row 12 As row 6.
Row 13 K2, p1, k1, p1, k3, p1, k1, p1, k2.
Row 14 P3, k1, p5, k1, p3.
These 14 rows form the heart motif panel.

Knit your right glove...
Using size 3 (3.25mm) needles and one strand of yarn, cast on 40 [44:48] sts loosely.
Row 1 *K1, p1; rep from * to end.
Rep this row until rib measures 2½in (6cm).
Change to size 6 (4mm) needles and work 2 rows in st st (1 row k, 1 row p), starting with a k row.**

Shape thumb gusset
Next Row K20 [22:24], M1, k2, M1, k18 [20:22]. 42 [46:50] sts.
Work 3 rows in st st.
Next Row K20 [22:24], M1, k4, M1, k18 [20:22]. 44 [48:52] sts.
Work 3 rows in st st.
Next Row K20 [22:24], M1, k6, M1, k18 [20:22]. 46 [50:54] sts.
Work 3 rows in st st.
Next Row K4 [5:6], work row 1 of heart motif panel, k3 [4:5], M1, k8, M1, k18 [20:22]. 48 [52:56] sts.
Next Row P31 [34:37], work row 2 of heart motif panel, p4 [5:6].

Next Row K4 [5:6], work row 3 of heart motif panel, k31 [34:37].
Next Row P31 [34:37] work row 4 of heart motif panel, p4 [5:6].
Next Row K4 [5:6], work row 5 of heart motif panel, k3 [4:5], M1, k10, M1, k18 [20:22]. 50 [54:58] sts.
Next Row P33 [36:39], work row 6 of heart motif panel, p4 [5:6].

Thumb
Next Row K4 [5:6], work row 7 of heart motif panel, k15 [16:17], and turn.
Next Row Cast on 2 sts (using cable cast-on – see page 103), p14 (including 2 sts just cast on), turn and cast on 2 sts.
***Work 2½ [2¾:3]in (6 [7:7.5]cm) on these 16 sts only for thumb, ending with a p row. Measure the knitting next to your thumb, placing cast-on sts at base of your thumb. You may need to add or subtract rows here to fit your thumb length.
Next Row K1, (k2tog, k1) 5 times. 11 sts.
P 1 row.
Next Row K1, (k2tog) 5 times.
Cut yarn and thread through rem 6 sts. Pull up tight and fasten off. Join thumb seam.
With RS of work facing, using size 6 (4mm) needles, pick up and k 2 sts across base of thumb, k across 18 [20:22] unworked sts on left-hand needle. 40 [44:48] sts.
****Keeping heart motif panel correct (beg with row 8), cont in st st without shaping until work measures 1½ [1¾:2]in (4 [4.5:5]cm) from pick-up sts at base of thumb, ending with a p row. Try the glove on; it should reach base of your fingers. You may need to add or subtract rows here to fit your hand length.

After working the st st for each finger, try the glove on and measure the knitting against your fingers. Adjust the length as required.

First finger

Next Row K25 [27:30] sts and turn.

Next Row Cast on 2 sts, p12 [12:14] (including 2 sts just cast on), turn and cast on 2 sts.

Work 2½in (6cm) on these 14 [14:16] sts only for first finger, ending with a p row.

Next Row K1, (k2tog, k1) 4 [4:5] times, k1 [1:0]. 10 [10:11] sts.

P 1 row.

Next Row K1, (k2tog) 4 [4:5] times, k1 [1:0]. Cut yarn and thread through rem 6 sts. Pull up tight and fasten off. Join finger seam.

Second finger

With RS of work facing, using size 6 (4mm) needles pick up and k 2 sts across base of first finger, k5 [6:6] sts and turn.

Next Row Cast on 1 st, p13 [15:15] (including st just cast on), turn and cast on 1 st.

Work 1in (7cm) on these 14 [16:16] sts only for second finger, ending with a p row.

Next Row K1, (k2tog, k1) 4 [5:5] times, k1 [0:0]. 10 [11:11] sts.

P 1 row.

Next Row K1, (k2tog) 4 [5:5] times, k1 [0:0]. Cut yarn and thread through rem 6 sts. Pull up tight and fasten off. Join finger seam.

Third finger

With RS of work facing, using size 6 (4mm) needles pick up and k 2 sts across base of second finger, k5 [6:6] sts and turn.

Next Row Cast on 1 st, p13 [15:15] (including st just cast on), turn and cast on 1 st.

Work 2½in (6cm) on these 14 [16:16] sts only for first finger, ending with a p row.

Next Row K1, (k2tog, k1) 4 [5:5] times, k1 [0:0]. 10 [11:11] sts.

P 1 row.

Next Row K1, (k2tog) 4 [5:5] times, k1 [0:0].

Cut yarn and thread through rem 6 sts. Pull up tight and fasten off. Join finger seam.

Fourth finger

With RS of work facing, using size 6 (4mm) needles, pick up and k 4 sts across base of third finger, k across 5 [5:6] unworked sts to end.

Next Row P across all 14 [14:16] rem sts.

Work 2in (5cm) on these 14 [14:16] sts only for fourth finger, ending with a p row.

Next Row K1, (k2tog, k1) 4 [4:5] times, k1 [1:0]. 10 [10:11] sts.

P 1 row.

Next Row K1, (k2tog) 4 [4:5] times, k1 [1:0]. Cut yarn and thread through rem 6 sts. Pull up tight and fasten off.

Knit your left glove...

Work as given for Right Glove to **.

Shape thumb gusset

Next Row K18 [20:22], M1, k2, M1, k20 [22:24]. 42 [46:50] sts.

Work 3 rows in st st.

Next Row K18 [20:22], M1, k4, M1, k20 [22:24]. 44 [48:52] sts.

Work 3 rows in st st.

Next Row K18 [20:22], M1, k6, M1, k20 [22:24]. 46 [50:54] sts.

Work 3 rows in st st.

Next Row K18 [20:22], M1, k8, M1, k3 [4:5], work row 1 of heart motif panel, k4 [5:6]. 48 [52:56] sts.

Next Row P4 [5:6], work row 2 of heart motif panel, p31 [34:37].

Next Row K31 [34:37], work row 3 of heart motif panel, k4 [5:6].

Next Row P4 [5:6], work row 4 of heart motif panel, p31 [34:37].

Next Row K18 [20:22], M1, k10, M1, k3 [4:5], work row 5 of heart motif panel, k4 [5:6]. 50 [54:58] sts.

Next Row P4 [5:6], work row 6 of heart motif panel, p33 [36:39].

Thumb

Next Row K30 [32:34] and turn.

Next Row Cast on 2 sts, p14 (including 2 sts just cast on), turn and cast on 2 sts.

Complete as given for Thumb of Right Glove from ***.

With RS of work facing, using size 6 (4mm) needles, pick up and k 2 sts across base of thumb, k3 [4:5], work row 7 of heart motif panel, k4 [5:6] across unworked sts on left-hand needle. 40 [44:48] sts.

Work as given for Right Glove from ****.

to finish...

Sew in all ends. Press pieces according to instructions on ball band. Join side seams.

mighty mitred squares

Mitred squares are really fun to knit and the geometric patterns look stunning. This scarf is made up of a repeat of two blocks of shapes. It looks as if there is a lot of sewing up involved, but there is surprisingly little. Each shape is worked by picking up stitches from the previous one. There are only a small number of stitches on your needle at any time. The instructions may seem complicated at first glance, but once you have your knitting needle in hand and work through the instructions, you will soon be hooked into this way of creating fabric.

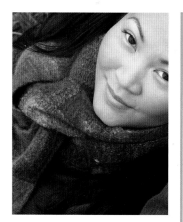

Fulling the scarf creates this beautifully dense yet soft fabric, which helps enhance the spectacular colour effects of the mitred squares.

YARN FOCUS

Mitred squares look best when worked in many colours. Instead of joining in a lot of different yarns, I used a multi-coloured wool yarn that would do that work for me. It is a fantastic bulky-weight (chunky) wool yarn in shades of green, pink and brown but with several other colours in there too. I needed a pure wool yarn because I intended to full this scarf when it was finished. The colours seem to merge with each other, producing a soft, brushed fabric.

DESIGN SECRETS UNRAVELLED...

If you want to full this scarf, choose a pure wool yarn or a yarn with a high wool content; these are the only yarns that will full. Test your yarn before you begin by fulling the gauge square. If you don't want to full the scarf, you could use any bulky-weight (chunky) multi-coloured yarn, or go through your stash and pick out a range of yarns to join together into a multi-yarn ball (see Beaded Beauties, pages 74–77). If you don't have enough bulky-weight yarns, mix two medium-weight (aran) yarns together or two light-weight (DK) and one medium-weight and add these to the ball. Remember to sew your ends in as you go.

mighty mitred squares

MEASUREMENTS
Before fulling: 6in (15cm) wide
by 72in (182cm) long
After fulling: 5½in (14cm) wide
by 66in (168cm) long

GATHER TOGETHER...
materials
6 x 1¾oz (50g) balls of bulky-weight (chunky)
wool multi-coloured yarn (109yd/100m per ball)
in green, pink and brown

needles and notions
1 pair of size 10 (6mm) needles
Stitch holders

GAUGE
16 sts and 20 rows to 4in (10cm) measured over
st st (1 row k, 1 row p) on size 10 (6mm) needles

knit note The edge stitches are important; you use them for picking up stitches for the next shape. Always slip the last stitch of every row purlwise with the yarn at the front of the work and always knit the slipped stitch on the return row.

knit note Use the cable cast-on method (see page 103) to cast on extra sts for the shape where indicated.

The shapes are decreased using k3tog (see page 111). Have two or three balls on the go at the same time; change over to start a new shape or block to keep the colours random and ensure a good contrast between shapes. The scarf is also fulled to create a unique fabric (see page 115).

Knit your first block...
Shape A1
Using size 10 (6mm) needles, cast on 15 sts loosely. (On subsequent blocks cast on 7 sts and pick up and knit 8 sts along edge of A2.)
Row 1 WS K14, sl 1.
Row 2 K6, k3tog, k5, sl 1. 13 sts.
Row 3 K1, p11, sl 1.
Row 4 K5, k3tog, k4, sl 1. 11 sts.
Row 5 K10, sl 1.
Row 6 K4, k3tog, k3, sl 1. 9 sts.
Row 7 K1, p7, sl 1.
Row 8 K3, k3tog, k2, sl 1. 7 sts.
Row 9 K6, sl 1.
Row 10 K2, k3tog, k1, sl 1. 5 sts.
Row 11 K1, p3, sl 1.
Row 12 K1, k3tog, sl 1. 3 sts.
Row 13 K2, sl 1.
Row 14 K3tog, leave this st on RH needle.

Shape B1
With RS of work facing, pick up and knit 7 sts down side of A1, swap needle into left hand and cast on 37 sts loosely. 45 sts. (On subsequent blocks, pick up and knit 7 sts down side of A1, 14 sts along edge of D2, sl st onto needle from stitch holder, swap needle into left hand and cast on 22 sts.)
Row 1 WS K44, sl 1.
Row 2 K6, k3tog, (k12, k3tog) twice, k5, sl 1. 39 sts.
Row 3 K1, p37, sl 1.
Row 4 K5, k3tog, (k10, k3tog) twice, k4, sl 1. 33 sts.
Row 5 K32, sl 1.
Row 6 K4, k3tog, (k8, k3tog) twice, k3, sl 1. 27 sts.
Row 7 K1, p25, sl 1.
Row 8 K3, k3tog, (k6, k3tog) twice, k2, sl 1. 21 sts.
Row 9 K20, sl 1.
Row 10 K2, k3tog, (k4, k3tog) twice, k1, sl 1. 15 sts.
Row 11 K1, p13, sl 1.

Row 12 K1, k3tog, (k2, k3tog) twice, sl 1. 9 sts.
Row 13 K8, sl 1.
Row 14 (K3tog) 3 times. 3 sts.
Row 15 P3tog. Cut yarn and leave rem st on a stitch holder.

Shape C1
With RS of work facing, pick up and knit 8 sts along top edge of B1, swap needle into left hand and cast on 7 sts loosely. 15 sts.
Work as given for A, cut yarn and leave rem st on a stitch holder.

Shape D1
With RS of work facing, pick up and knit 8 sts along top edge of A1, 7 sts along edge of B1, sl st onto needle from stitch holder, 7 sts along second edge of B1, 7 sts along edge of C1 and sl st onto needle from stitch holder. 31 sts.
Row 1 WS K30, sl 1.
Row 2 K14, k3tog, k13, sl 1. 29 sts.
Row 3 K1, p27, sl 1.
Row 4 K13, k3tog, k12, sl 1. 27 sts.
Row 5 K26, sl 1.
Row 6 K12, k3tog, k11, sl 1. 25 sts.
Row 7 K1, p23, sl 1.
Row 8 K11, k3tog, k10, sl 1. 23 sts.
Row 9 K22, sl 1.
Row 10 K10, k3tog, k9, sl 1. 21 sts.
Row 11 K1, p19, sl 1.
Row 12 K9, k3tog, k8, sl 1. 19 sts.
Row 13 K18, sl 1.
Row 14 K8, k3tog, k7, sl 1. 17 sts.
Row 15 K1, p15, sl 1.
Row 16 K7, k3tog, k6, sl 1. 15 sts.
Row 17 K14, sl 1.
Row 18 K6, k3tog, k5, sl 1. 13 sts.
Row 19 K1, p11, sl 1.

Row 20 K5, k3tog, k4, sl 1. 11 sts.
Row 21 K10, sl 1.
Row 22 K4, k3tog, k3, sl 1. 9 sts.
Row 23 K1, p7, sl 1.
Row 24 K3, k3tog, k2, sl 1. 7 sts.
Row 25 K6, sl 1.
Row 26 K2, k3tog, k1, sl 1. 5 sts.
Row 27 K1, p3, sl 1.
Row 28 K1, k3tog, sl 1. 3 sts.
Row 29 K2, sl 1.
Row 30 K3tog, cut yarn and leave rem st on a stitch holder.
First block completed.

knit your second block...

Second block is worked on top of first block as follows:

Work shape A2 as given for A1.

Work shape B2 as follows: with RS of work facing, pick up and knit 7 sts down side of A2, swap needle into left hand and cast on 14 sts loosely, swap needle back into right hand, sl st onto needle from stitch holder at D1, pick up and knit 15 sts along edge of D1, swap needle back into left hand and cast on 7 sts. 45 sts.
Complete as given for B1.

Work shape C2 as follows: with RS of work facing, pick up and knit 8 sts down side of B2, and 7 sts along edge of C1. 15 sts.
Complete as given for C1.

Work D2 as given for D1, picking up sts around A2, B2 and C2.

Repeat first and second blocks 5 times more. Scarf measures approx 72in (162cm).

To finish...

Sew in all ends. Follow the instructions on page 115 to full the scarf.

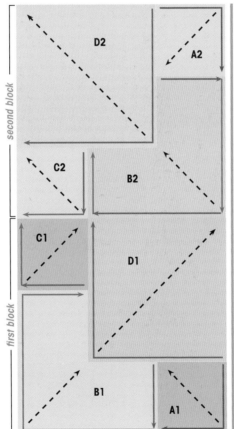

→ *cast on stitches*
→ *pick up stitches*
- -→ *direction of knitting*

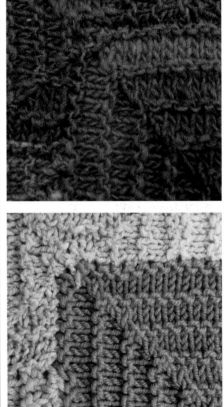

DESIGN SECRETS UNRAVELLED...

The blue/green swatch above is knitted in the same yarn as the scarf, but has been left unfulled. The garter-stitch ridges are clearer and the finished square is bigger, so the completed scarf would be wider. The swatch beneath shows how you could use several different yarns together to create a more patchwork effect. I chose shades of green, but you could choose different textures of the same colour. Choose yarns that are a similar weight.

weekender cap

I wanted this cap to look like an old pair of jeans; casual, worn in and starting to fray on the seams. The cap is knitted in eight sections that are then sewn together with the seams on the outside, adding to the casual look. Each section is shaped using k2tog, ssk and finally sl2tog-k1-psso. The stitches for the brim are picked up around the edge; the brim itself is shaped using ssk, k2tog and ssp and p2tog (all these decreasing methods are explained fully on pages 110–111).

The fit of this fun casual cap is achieved by knitting each section separately and sewing them together.

DESIGN SECRETS UNRAVELLED...

Denim yarns are available in a range of shades from light to dark blue. You could knit each section in a different shade to create a patched look, or knit the underside of the brim in a darker shade than the cap. If you can't find a denim yarn, you could mix your own with two light-weight (DK) cotton yarns in ecru and blue, or a variegated blue would be even better. You could use a mix of cotton yarns; bright pinks, dark purples, sunny yellows and oranges for summer. Add an appliqué patch or sew beads and sequins into flower shapes. Alternatively, knit one of the flowers on page 121 in denim yarn to match.

YARN FOCUS

I wanted to use a denim yarn for this cap, but not one that would shrink when it was washed, as many of them do. This medium-weight (aran) yarn is a great-looking yarn, being a mix of denim blue and ecru just like a pair of jeans. When the ends are cut they fray a little, so you need not be too meticulous with your sewing in.

weekender cap

MEASUREMENTS

To fit head circumference 20in [22in] (51 [56]cm)

GATHER TOGETHER...
materials

3 x 1¾oz (50g) balls of medium-weight (aran) cotton yarn (74yd/68m per ball) in denim blue

needles

1 pair of size 5 (3.75mm) needles
1 pair of size 7 (4.5mm) needles

GAUGE

18 sts and 24 rows to 4in (10cm) measured over st st (1 row k, 1 row p) using size 7 (4.5mm) needles

The shaping in this dressed-down, casual cap is achieved by knitting each section individually and sewing the pieces together. Don't be put off if you think your sewing skills are not up to the task; see pages 116–117 for further advice on finishing techniques.

Knit your cap section (make 8)...

Using size 5 (3.75mm) needles, cast on 13 [14] sts.
Work 6 rows in st st (1 row k, 1 row p) beg with a k row.
Change to size 7 (4.5mm) needles.
Inc Row K2 [1], M1, (k3, M1) 3 [4] times, k2 [1]. 17 [19] sts.
Work 19 rows in st st, beg with a p row.

2nd size only
Next Row K1, k2tog, k13, ssk, k1. 17 sts.
Work 3 rows.

Both sizes
Next Row K1, k2tog, k11, ssk, k1. 15 sts.
Work 3 rows.
Next Row K1, k2tog, k9, ssk, k1. 13 sts.
Work 3 rows.
Next Row K1, k2tog, k7, ssk, k1. 11 sts.
Work 3 rows.
Next Row K1, k2tog, k5, ssk, k1. 9 sts.
Work 3 rows.
Next Row K1, k2tog, k3, ssk, k1. 7 sts.
P 1 row.
Next Row K1, k2tog, k1, ssk, k1. 5 sts.
P 1 row.
Next Row K1, sl2tog-k1-psso, k1. 3 sts.
Next Row P3tog.
Cut yarn and draw through last st.

to finish...

Sew in all ends. Press pieces according to instructions on ball band. Sew the eight sections together with the seams on the outside.

Upper brim
With RS of work facing and using size 7 (4.5mm) needles, and starting at a seam, pick up and knit 33 sts evenly across 3 sections.
P 1 row.
**Inc Row K2, k into front and back of next st, (k1, k into front and back of next st) 4 times, k11, k into front and back of next st, (k1, k into front and back of next st) 4 times, k2. 43 sts.
P 1 row.
Next Row K1, ssk, k to last 3 sts, k2tog, k1. 41 sts.
Next Row P1, p2tog, p to last 3 sts, ssp, p1. 39 sts.
Dec 2 sts as set on every row to 25 sts, ending with a k row.
Bind off.***

Lower brim
Using size 7 (4.5mm) needles, cast on 33 sts and p 1 row.
Work as given for Upper Brim from ** to ***.

Sew in all ends. Press the brim sections according to instructions on ball band. Place the lower brim under the upper brim with WS together. Stitch them together. Sew the lower brim to the cap.

new yarn, new look!

I found this fantastic green yarn in the baby wool section, hiding among the pastels. There are hidden gems to be found everywhere; explore every corner of your local yarn shop. The yarn looked to me like camouflage, so I thought it would work well as an urban take on the casual weekender cap. To make up the medium-weight (aran) yarn I needed, I mixed it with a copper metallic yarn for a flash of glamour. As an alternative, work each section of the weekender cap in a different tweed. I made up my own selection of tweed yarns by collecting together a few light-weight (DK) yarns in shades of purple. I knitted each one together with a fine-weight (4ply) tweed yarn in grey; this yarn adds a common colour to all the sections of the cap, merging them together. Use solid shades and self-striping or textured and flat yarns.

IN THE MIX

Urban cap

A Light-weight (DK) yarn with snarl and slub twist (90% acrylic/10% polyester – 150yd/137m per ball) in olive green

B Fine-weight (4ply) metallic yarn (80% viscose/20% polyester – 104yd/95m per ball) in copper

Tweed cap

A Fine-weight (4ply) tweed wool (100% wool – 120yd/110m per ball) in grey

B light-weight (DK) wool (100% wool – 131yd/120m per ball) in dark purple

C light-weight (DK) wool (100% merino wool – 131yd/120m per ball) in self-striping light to dark purple

D fine-weight (4ply) Shetland wool (100% Shetland wool – 129yd/118m per ball) in purple

AND IT DOESN'T END THERE...

Instead of a purple mix for the tweed cap, how about shades of brown with a cream yarn, or shades of red with bronze? Make sure each of your yarn mixes knit up to the correct gauge.

91

magic mitten gloves

These two-way gloves combine the versatility of fingerless gloves and the warmth of mittens. The gloves are knitted in the same way as those on pages 32–43, but the fingers and thumb are bound off after 1in (2.5cm). The thumb gusset is increased out from the hand using M1 (see page 108). The stitches for the mitten flap are picked up along the back of the hand, and the top is shaped using ssk and k2tog, and k3tog and k3tog tbl (see pages 110–111). The main project has been worked in different colours, but the variation shown on page 95 shows how changing the yarn can make a dramatic difference. The technique of knitting gloves is explained on page 113.

Working each mitten finger in a different complementary colour adds a pleasingly quirky detail to these versatile gloves.

DESIGN SECRETS UNRAVELLED...

You don't have to knit these gloves in as many colours; you could knit them in one colour throughout. Alternatively, you could work the glove in one colour and the mitten flap in another, or just the rib cuff in a contrasting colour. Add a special button, or bead for embellishment. Sew an appliqué patch onto the back of the flap or Swiss darn (see page 118) a heart motif that will only be revealed when the gloves are worn as mittens.

YARN FOCUS

Gloves are most successful when knitted in light-weight (DK) yarns. The shaping is quite important and anything thicker would appear clumsy. This yarn is a great 100% wool yarn in the right weight and knits up in stockinette stitch beautifully. I chose a selection of rich, autumnal colours that would look great throughout the winter.

falling for you gloves

You can never have too many pairs of gloves; they're warm, practical, and add colour to whatever you're wearing. They don't take up much yarn, so are a satisfying quick knit and a good way of using up oddments of yarn.

MEASUREMENTS

To fit sizes S [M:L]; width around palm is 7 [8:8½]in (18 [20.5:22]cm) and 7 [7½:8]in (18 [19:20.5]cm) long from wrist to top of mitten flap

GATHER TOGETHER...
materials

1 x 1¾oz (50g) light-weight (DK) wool yarn (131yd/120m per ball) in each of colours pumpkin (A), green (B), gold (C), yellow (D) and russet red (E)

2 x small buttons

needles and notions

1 pair of size 3 (3.25mm) needles
1 pair of size 6 (4mm) needles
Stitch markers

GAUGE

22 sts and 28 rows to 4in (10cm) measured over st st (1 row k, 1 row p) using size 6 (4mm) needles

Knit your right glove...

Using size 3 (3.25mm) needles and A, cast on 40 [44:48] sts loosely.

Row 1 *K1, p1; rep from * to end.

Rep this row until rib measures 2½in (6cm). Change to size 6 (4mm) needles and B. Work 2 rows in st st (1 row k, 1 row p), starting with a k row.**

Shape thumb gusset

Next Row K20 [22:24], M1, k2, M1, k18 [20:22]. 42 [46:50] sts.

Work 3 rows in st st.

Next Row K20 [22:24], M1, k4, M1, k18 [20:22]. 44 [48:52] sts.

Work 3 rows in st st.

Next Row K20 [22:24], M1, k6, M1, k18 [20:22]. 46 [50:54] sts.

Work 3 rows in st st.

Next Row K20 [22:24], M1, k8, M1, k18 [20:22]. 48 [52:56] sts.

Work 3 rows in st st.

Next Row K20 [22:24], M1, k10, M1, k18 [20:22]. 50 [54:58] sts.

Purl 1 row.

Thumb

Next Row K32 [34:36] and turn.

Next Row Using C, cast on 2 sts (using cable cast-on – see page 103), p14 (including last 2 sts just cast on), turn and cast on 2 sts.

Using C, work 1in (2.5cm) on these 16 sts only for thumb, ending with a p row.

Bind off loosely. Join thumb seam.

With RS of work facing, using size 6 (4mm) needles and B, pick up and k 2 sts across base of thumb, k across 18 [20:22] unworked sts on left-hand needle. 40 [44:48] sts.

Work 2 rows. Place markers on the 2nd and 19th

[21st:23rd] sts of the last row.

***Cont in st st without shaping until work measures 1½ [1½:2]in (4 [4.5:5]cm) from pick-up sts at base of thumb, ending with a p row. Try the glove on; it should reach the base of your fingers. You may need to add or subtract rows here to fit your hand length.

First finger

Next Row K25 [27:30] sts and turn.

Next Row Using D, cast on 2 sts, p12 [12:14] (including 2 sts just cast on), turn and cast on 2 sts.

Using D, work 1in (2.5cm) on these 14 [14:16] sts only for first finger, ending with a p row.

Bind off loosely. Join finger seam.

Second finger

With RS of work facing, using size 6 (4mm) needles and C, pick up and k 2 sts across base of first finger, k5 [6:6] and turn.

Next Row Cast on 1 st, p13 [15:15] (including st just cast on), turn and cast on 1 st.

Using C, work 1in (2.5cm) on these 14 [16:16] sts only for second finger, ending with a p row.

Bind off loosely. Join finger seam.

Third finger

With RS of work facing, using size 6 (4mm) needles and A, pick up and k 2 sts across base of second finger, k5 [6:6] and turn.

Next Row Cast on 1 st, p13 [15:15] (including st just cast on), turn and cast on 1 st.

Using A, work 1in (2.5cm) on these 14 [16:16] sts only for third finger, ending with a p row.

Bind off loosely. Join finger seam.

Fourth finger

With RS of work facing, using size 6 (4mm) needles and E, pick up and k 4 sts across base of

third finger, k across 5 [5:6] unworked sts to end.
Next Row P across all 14 [14:16] rem sts.
Using E, work 1in (2.5cm) on these 14 [14:16] sts only for fourth finger, ending with a p row.
Bind off loosely. Join finger seam.

Mitten flap

Using size 3 (3.25mm) needles and E, cast on 20 [22:24] sts loosely.
Row 1 *K1, p1; rep from * to end.
Rep this row 3 times more.
Leave these sts on a spare needle.
With RS of work facing, using size 6 (4mm) needles and D, cast on 1 st then pick up and k 18 [20:22] sts between markers on back of glove. 19 [21:23] sts.
P 1 row.
Next Row K19 [21:23] then k across 20 [22:24] sts of rib from spare needle. 39 [43:47] sts.
****Work in st st until flap measures 2½ [3½:3½]in (6cm) from pick-up row, ending with a p row. Try the glove on; the flap should be 1in (2.5cm) below the top of your longest finger. Add or subtract rows to fit your hand length if necessary.

Shape top

Next Row K1, ssk, k14 [16:18], k3tog, ssk, k14 [16:18], k2tog, k1. 34 [38:42] sts.
P 1 row.
Next Row K1, (ssk, k12 [14:16], k2tog) twice, k1. 30 [34:38] sts.
P 1 row.
Next Row K1, (ssk, k10 [12:14], k2tog) twice, k1. 26 [30:34]sts.
P 1 row.
Next Row K1, (k3tog tbl, k6 [8:10], k3tog) twice, k1. 18 [22:26] sts.
Bind off.

Knit your left glove...

Work as given for Right Glove to **.

Shape thumb gusset

Next Row K18 [20:22], M1, k2, M1, k20 [22:24]. 42 [46:50] sts.

Work 3 rows in st st.
Next Row K18 [20:22], M1, k4, M1, k20 [22:24]. 44 [48:52] sts.
Work 3 rows in st st.
Next Row K18 [20:22], M1, k6, M1, k20 [22:24]. 46 [50:54] sts.
Work 3 rows in st st.
Next Row K18 [20:22], M1, k8, M1, k20 [22:24]. 48 [52:56] sts.
Work 3 rows in st st.
Next Row K18 [20:22], M1, k10, M1, k20 [22:24]. 50 [54:58] sts.
Purl 1 row.

Thumb

Next Row K30 [32:34] and turn.
Next Row Using C, cast on 2 sts (using cable cast-on), p14 (including last 2 sts just cast on), turn and cast on 2 sts.
Using C, work 1in (2.5cm) on these 16 sts only for thumb, ending with a p row.
Bind off loosely. Join thumb seam.
With RS of work facing using size 6 (4mm) needles and B, pick up and k 2 sts across base of thumb, k 20 [22:24] unworked sts on left-hand needle. 40 [44:48] sts.
Work 2 rows. Place markers on the 22nd [24th:26th] and 39th [43rd:47th] sts of the last row.
Work as given for Right Glove from ***.

Mitten flap

Using size 3 (3.25mm) needles and E, cast on 20 [22:24] sts loosely.
Row 1 *K1, p1; rep from * to end.
Rep this row 3 times more.
Leave these sts on a spare needle.
With RS of work facing, using size 6 (4mm) needles and D, pick up and k 18 [20:22] sts between markers on back of glove.
Next Row Cast on 1 st, p to end. 19 [21:22] sts.
K 1 row.
Next Row P19 [21:23] then p across 20 [22:24] sts of rib from spare needle. 39 [43:47] sts.
Complete as given for Mitten Flap of Right Glove from ****.

to finish...

Sew in all yarn ends. Join top seam of mitten flap. Join side seam of flap to top of rib. Sew each end of the rib flat onto the glove. Join side seam of glove. Make a small loop in the middle of the top of the flap, using 2 strands of D. Work buttonhole stitch evenly over the loop. Fold the flap over onto the back of glove, mark the position of the loop and sew on a small button.

Soft 'n' subtle

I wanted to show these gloves in a totally different way, which I achieved using a mix of two shades of the same yarn; 1 x 1¾oz (50g) ball of fine-weight (4ply) cotton/angora/cashmere mix yarn (197yd/180m per ball) in each of pale blue and sea green. They combine to produce a subtle marled fabric while still knitting up to the correct gauge. This version is worked in a mix of two fine-weight (4ply) yarns. Work as given for multi-coloured version using one strand of each colour held together throughout – make sure that you work through both yarns for each stitch.

Alternatively, you could use one wool and one mohair yarn for cosiness, or one silk yarn for luxury. Add a metallic thread for sparkle, or a bouclé yarn for texture.

crossover cables

These projects show what different effects you can achieve with cabling depending on the weight of yarn that you use. Two panels of cables make up the more traditional poncho (shown opposite), which is worked in a heavy yarn, while only one is used for the more unusual light-weight wrap (shown on page 101). There is no shaping; you just cast on and work a thick centre cable with a smaller cable on each side. The cable panels uses C6F, C6B, Cr4L, and Cr4R (see page 112) to cross the stitches; it is a simple 18-row pattern that you will soon learn.

The variegated and muted natural colours of this thick yarn enhance the earthy organic style of this chunky cabled poncho.

DESIGN SECRETS UNRAVELLED...

These two medium-weight (aran) yarns together knit up to a bulky-weight (chunky) gauge. You could choose a handspun yarn with slubs and bumps for a really fantastic thick and textural fabric. Or you could make up a mix of thinner yarns such as two light-weight (DK) wools with a medium-weight (aran) tweed, or a light-weight (DK) mohair and three shades of light-weight (DK) wool. Go for big yarns with big personalities and this poncho will knit up in no time.

YARN FOCUS

I wanted this poncho to be almost like a blanket; very thick, warm and heavy. I chose to knit it in a medium-weight (aran) multi-coloured wool yarn in shades of green and brown. However, this wasn't thick enough to achieve the look I wanted, so I used two strands together to create this fantastic bulky cable and fabric.

classic cabled poncho

MEASUREMENTS

74in (188cm) circumference at widest point and 21in (53.5cm) long on shoulder (when worn as a poncho with point at centre front and back)

GATHER TOGETHER...
materials

11 x 3½oz (100g) hanks of medium-weight (aran) multi-coloured wool yarn (150yd/138m per hank) in shades of green

needles and notions

1 pair of size 13 (9mm) needles
Cable needle
Stitch markers

GAUGE

10 sts and 12 rows to 4in (10cm) measured over st st using size 13 (9mm) needles and two strands of yarn together

knit note Two yarns are used together to make a thicker yarn. Make sure that you work through both yarns for each stitch.

Special Abbreviations

C6F   slip next 3 sts onto a cable needle at front of work, k3, then k3 from cable needle.

C6B   slip next 3 sts onto a cable needle at back of work, k3, then k3 from cable needle.

Cr4L slip next 3 sts onto a cable needle at front of work, p1, then k3 from cable needle.

Cr4R slip next st onto a cable needle at back of work, k3, then p1 from cable needle.

Knitting the cable panels
Throughout the project pattern you will have to refer back to these instructions for knitting cable panels A, B and C:

CABLE PANEL A (10 STS)
Row 1 RS P2, C6B, p2.
Row 2 K2, p6, k2.
Row 3 P2, k6, p2.
Row 4 As row 2.
Row 5 As row 3.
Row 6 K2, p6, k2.

CABLE PANEL B (24 STS)
Row 1 RS P4, C6B, p4, C6F, p4.
Row 2 (K4, p6) twice, k4.
Row 3 P3, Cr4R, Cr4L, p2, Cr4R, Cr4L, p3.
Row 4 K3, (p3, k2) 3 times, p3, k3.
Row 5 P2, (Cr4R, p2, Cr4L) twice, p2.
Row 6 K2, p3, k4, p6, k4, p3, k2.
Row 7 P2, k3, p4, C6F, p4, k3, p2.

Row 8 As row 6.
Row 9 P2, k3, p4, k6, p4, k3, p2.
Row 10 As row 6.
Row 11 As row 9.
Row 12 As row 6.
Row 13 As row 7.
Row 14 As row 6.
Row 15 P2, (Cr4L, p2, Cr4R) twice, p2.
Row 16 As row 4.
Row 17 P3, Cr4L, Cr4R, p2, Cr4L, Cr4R, p3.
Row 18 (K4, p6) twice, k4.

CABLE PANEL C (10 STS)
Row 1 RS P2, C6F, p2.
Row 2 K2, p6, k2.
Row 3 P2, k6, p2.
Row 4 As row 2.
Row 5 As row 3.

Cables are historically associated with sturdy woollens such as bulky fishermen's sweaters. The cabled panels on this poncho work well used in this traditional way; they lend a pleasingly solid and chunky detail to the wonderfully warm garment.

Knit your poncho...

Work two pieces the same.
Using size 13 (9mm) needles and two strands of yarn together, cast on 65 sts loosely.
Row 1 RS K1, *p1, k1; rep from * to end.
Row 2 P1, *k1, p1; rep from * to end.
Row 3 As row 2.
Inc Row (K1, p1) 7 times, M1, k1, (p1, k1) 6 times, M1, (p1, k1, p1, M1, k1, p1, k1, M1) twice, (p1, k1) 6 times, M1, (p1, k1) 7 times. 72 sts.
Foundation Row 1 (K1, p1) twice, k5, p2, k6, p2, k5, (p4, k6) twice, p4, k5, p2, k6, p2, k5, (p1, k1) twice.
Foundation Row 2 (P1, k1) twice, p5, k2, p6, k2, p5, (k4, p6) twice, k4, p5, k2, p6, k2, p5, (k1, p1) twice.
Beg moss (UK: double moss) stitch edges and panels.
Row 1 (P1, k1) twice, k5, work 1st row of panel A, k5, work 1st row of panel B, k5, work 1st row of panel C, k5, (k1, p1) twice.
Row 2 (K1, p1) twice, p5, work 2nd row of panel C, p5, work 2nd row of panel B, p5, work 2nd row of panel A, p5, (p1, k1) twice.
Row 3 (K1, p1) twice, k5, work 3rd row of panel A, k5, work 3rd row of panel B, k5, work 3rd row of panel C, k5, (p1, k1) twice.
Row 4 (P1, k1) twice, p5, work 4th row of panel C, p5, work 4th row of panel B, p5, work 4th row of panel A, p5, (k1, p1) twice.
These 4 rows form moss (double moss) stitch borders and set cable panels A, B and C.**

Cont in patt as set, starting with 5th row of panels A, B and C, until 6 repeats of panel B have been worked, ending with row 18.

Next Row (P1, k1) twice, k5, work 1st row of panel A, k5, work 1st row of panel B, k5, work 1st row of panel C, k5, (k1, p1) twice.

Dec Row Patt 13 sts, p2tog, patt 11 sts, (k2tog, patt 2 sts, p2tog, patt 2 sts) twice, p2tog, patt 13 sts, p2tog, patt to end. 65 sts.

Work 3 rows in moss (double moss) stitch.

Bind off loosely in patt.

To finish...

Sew in all ends. Block each piece to measure 33in (84cm) long and 21in (54cm) wide. The two pieces are joined together to form a poncho as follows: with RS of work facing, place a marker on the right-hand side edge of one piece 21in (54cm) up from cast-on edge. Sew the bound-off edge of the second piece along the side of first piece from cast-on to marker. With RS of work facing, place a marker on the right-hand side edge of the second piece 21in (54cm) up from cast-on edge. Sew the bound-off edge of the first piece along the side of second piece from cast-on to marker.

This poncho has been sewn together to create a neck opening. If you prefer to wear it as a wrap, simply knit one piece as long as you want it.

cobweb cabled wrap

MEASUREMENTS

Wrap measures 21in (54cm) wide by 86in (218cm) long

GATHER TOGETHER...

materials

9 x $\frac{7}{8}$oz (25g) balls of super-fine-weight mohair/silk mix yarn (229yd/210m per ball) in shaded berry red

needles and notions

1 pair of size 13 (9mm) needles
Cable needle

GAUGE

10 sts and 13 rows to 4in (10cm) measured over st st using size 13 (9mm) needles and three strands of yarn together.

knit note *Three yarns are used together to make a thicker yarn. Make sure that you work through all three yarns for each stitch.*

Cables are not often used with light-weight yarns, but why not try something different? The cabling does not stand out so clearly on this fine and hairy yarn, and yet it creates a beautiful and unique texture in this soft and airy fabric.

Knit your wrap...

Make one panel as given for poncho to **.

Cont in patt as set, starting with 5th row of panels A, B and C, until 14 repeats of panel B have been worked, ending with row 18.

Next Row (P1, k1) twice, k5, work 1st row of panel A, k5, work 1st row of panel B, k5, work 1st row of panel C, k5, (k1, p1) twice.

Dec Row Patt 13 sts, p2tog, patt 11 sts, (k2tog, patt 2 sts, p2tog, patt 2 sts) twice, p2tog, patt 13 sts, p2tog, patt to end. 65 sts.

Work 3 rows in moss (UK: double moss) stitch.

Bind off loosely in patt.

to finish...

Sew in all yarn ends. Block wrap to measure 21in (54cm) wide and 86in (218cm) long.

YARN FOCUS

I wanted this to be a total contrast to the poncho. I used three strands of a super-fine-weight mohair and silk mix yarn in shaded berry colours. This produces a very light and airy fabric when knitted on large needles. If you want a wrap with a little more weight, how about working one in a cotton and silk mix yarn for summer evenings? Use two medium-weight (aran) yarns for a substantial wrap or two light-weight (DK) yarns for a lighter one. Try it in tweed wool for a fantastic winter wrap or mix up a yarn in brilliant shades of gold and orange for the autumn. Make sure that your final mix knits up to the correct gauge.

it's all in
the detail...

casting on

Most knitters have their own favoured method for casting on, so I have generally not specified which method to use – with the exception of the few projects where the cable cast-on (explained below) is recommended. In many of the projects I have added the instruction to cast on loosely, especially for the hats. If you cast on too tightly, the edge will not stretch sufficiently and may break. Try using a size larger needle to make sure it is loose enough. Remember to change back to the correct size needle to begin knitting.

CABLE CAST-ON

This method of casting on is used when making the gloves and mittens, and also for the Mighty Mitred Squares (see pages 84–87) because the stitches can be cast on at the beginning or in the middle of a row. This method needs two needles.

To cast on at the beginning of a project, make a slip knot about 6in (15cm) from the end of the yarn and slip it on to a needle held in your left hand.

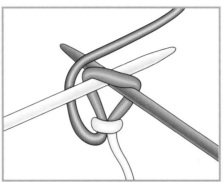

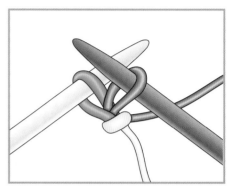

1 Insert the right-hand needle into the slip knot as though to knit it and wrap the yarn around the tip.

2 Pull a new loop through but do not slip the stitch off the left-hand needle.

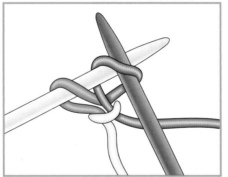

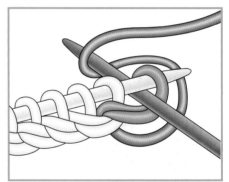

3 Place the loop on to the left-hand needle by inserting the left-hand needle into the front of the loop from right to left.

4 Insert the right-hand needle between the two stitches and wrap the yarn around the tip. When the new loop is pulled through between the stitches, place it on the left-hand needle, as shown in step 3.

Repeat step 4 until you have cast on the required number of stitches.

Extra stitches

To cast on the extra stitches needed in the middle of knitting, work step 4 only, working the first stitch between the next two stitches already on the left-hand needle.

knit stitch

The knit stitch is the classic knitting stitch, and the one that all beginners learn first. Once you know this stitch, you can start making fabulous accessories; all the glamorous items shown on pages 20–27 were made using just the knit stitch.

GARTER STITCH

When you knit each row, the fabric you make is called garter stitch (g st) and has rows of raised ridges on the front and back of the fabric. It looks the same on the back and the front so it is reversible. Garter stitch lies flat, is quite a thick fabric and does not curl at the edges, which is why I have used it for the scarves and the wrap on pages 20–27.

MAKING THE KNIT STITCH

Each knit stitch is made up of four easy steps. The yarn is held at the back of the work (the side facing away from you).

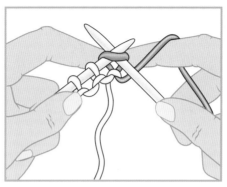

1 Hold the needle with the cast-on stitches in your left hand, and insert the right-hand needle into the front of the stitch from left to right.

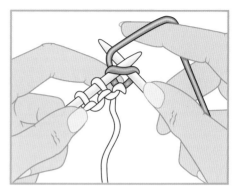

2 Pass the yarn under and around the right-hand needle.

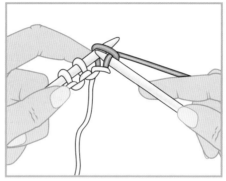

3 Pull the new loop on the right-hand needle through the stitch on the left-hand needle.

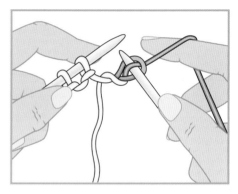

4 Slip the stitch off the left-hand needle. One knit stitch is completed.

Repeat these four steps for each stitch on the left-hand needle. All the stitches on the left-hand needle will be transferred to the right-hand needle, where the new row is formed. At the end of the row, swap the needle with the stitches into your left hand and the empty needle into your right hand to begin the next row.

purl stitch

Purl stitch is the other classic knitting stitch. Once you know both the knit and purl stitches, you can pretty much make anything. One row of knit and one row of purl makes stockinette stitch, which, with its clearly distinguishable right and wrong side, forms the fundamental knitted fabric.

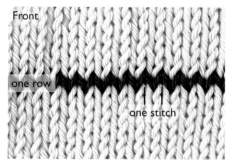

STOCKINETTE STITCH

Stockinette stitch (st st) is formed by knitting one row, purling the next row, and then repeating these two rows.
In the knitting instructions for the projects, stockinette stitch is written as follows:

Row 1 RS Knit.

Row 2 Purl.

Or, the instructions may be:

Work in st st (1 row k, 1 row p), beg with a k row.

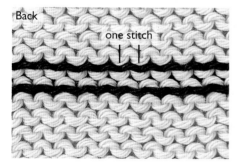

REVERSE STOCKINETTE STITCH

Reverse stockinette stitch (rev st st) is when the back of stockinette stitch fabric is used as the right side. This is commonly used as the background for cables, but can also be used as the right side of fabrics knitted in fancy yarns, such as faux fur or fashion yarns. This is because most of the textured effect of the yarn remains on the reverse side of the fabric.

MAKING THE PURL STITCH

Each purl stitch is made up of four easy steps. The yarn is held at the front of the work (the side facing you).

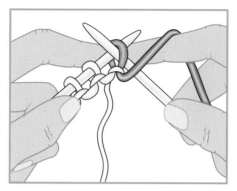

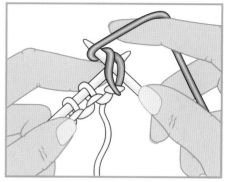

1 Hold the needle with the cast-on stitches in your left hand, and insert the right-hand needle into the front of the stitch from right to left.

2 Pass the yarn over and around the right-hand needle.

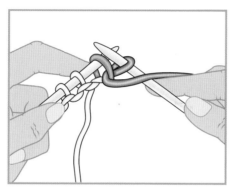

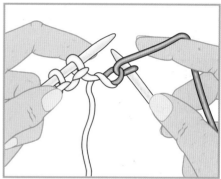

3 Pull the new loop on the right-hand needle through the stitch on the left-hand needle.

4 Slip the stitch off the left-hand needle. One stitch is completed.

Repeat these four steps for each stitch on the left-hand needle. All the stitches on the left-hand needle will be transferred to the right-hand needle, where the new purl row is formed. At the end of the row, swap the needle with the stitches into your left hand and the empty needle into your right hand to begin the next row.

binding off

Unless specifically instructed to do otherwise, you should bind off in pattern – for example, bind off knitwise on the right side of a piece knitted in stockinette stitch. The various methods are explained below. The bound-off edge should not be too tight otherwise it will pull the knitted fabric in. This is important when binding off a visible edge, such as the edge of a scarf or poncho. If you do tend to bind off tightly, try using a needle a size larger than that used for the knitted fabric.

BIND OFF KNITWISE

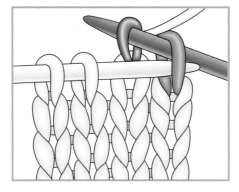

1 Knit two stitches, and insert the tip of the left-hand needle into the front of the first stitch on the right-hand needle.

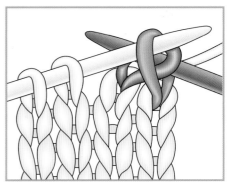

2 Lift this stitch over the second stitch and off the needle.

KNIT PERFECT

When you wish to stop knitting, bur aren't ready to bind off yet, always finish the complete row. Finishing in the middle of a row will stretch the stitches and they may slide off the needle. If you need to put your knitting aside for several weeks or even months and do not have time to finish the piece beforehand, mark on the pattern or make a note of where you have got to. If you are working in a regular pattern such as stockinette stitch, when restarting again it is worth unravelling a couple of rows and reknitting them, as stitches left over time on the needles can become stretched and leave an unsightly ridge where you stopped.

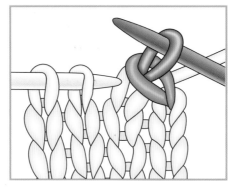

3 One stitch is left on the right-hand needle.

4 Knit the next stitch and lift the second stitch over this and off the needle. Continue in this way until one stitch remains on the right-hand needle.

Cut the yarn (leaving a length long enough to sew in), thread the end through the last stitch and slip it off the needle. Pull the yarn end to tighten the stitch.

BIND OFF PURLWISE

To bind off on a purl row, simply purl the stitches instead of knitting them.

BIND OFF IN PATTERN

To bind off in rib, you must knit the knit stitches and purl the purl stitches of the rib. If you are working a pattern of cable stitches, you bind off in pattern; again, knit the knit stitches and purl the purl stitches.

weaving in yarn ends

This is a great time-saving technique; weave your yarn ends in as you knit. It produces a neat finish when changing colours for stripes or when using multi-yarn balls.

In a design that uses lots of different yarns, such as the Beaded Beauties scarves (pages 74–77), you will get a lot of ends of yarn where they have been joined. Weaving these ends in as you knit will save you the long and arduous job of sewing them in.

Weaving in ends on a knit row

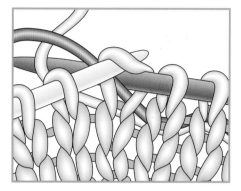

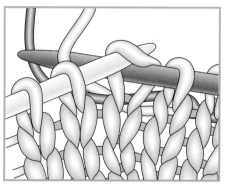

1 Insert the tip of the right-hand needle into the next stitch, bring the cut end over the needle, wrap the yarn around the needle as though to knit.

2 Pull the cut end off the needle and finish knitting the stitch. The cut end is caught into the knitted stitch.

Work the next stitch as normal, then catch the cut end in as before. If you work alternately like this the cut end will lie above and below the row of stitches.

Weaving in ends on a purl row

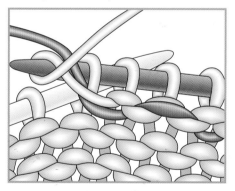

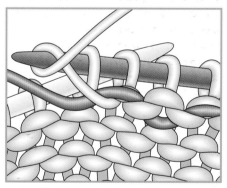

1 Insert the tip of the right-hand needle into the next stitch, bring the cut end over the needle, wrap the yarn around the needle as though to purl.

2 Pull the cut end off the needle and finish purling the stitch. The cut end is caught into the purled stitch.

Work the next stitch as normal, then catch the cut end in as before. If you work alternately like this the cut end will lie above and below the row of stitches.

KNIT PERFECT

If you are working with two colours or with two balls of the same yarn (as recommended for multi-coloured yarns), instead of cutting yarn and joining in the new yarn, carry the yarn not in use up the side of the work.

To change yarns every two yarns:
Bring the new yarn B in front of the old yarn A and continue to work with B.
Bring A in front of B and continue to work with A. By always bringing the new yarn up in front of the old yarn, you create a neat edge.

You can carry a yarn up more than two rows. The Making Waves Scarf (pages 54–57) has four rows of A and four rows of B worked alternately. Instead of leaving long loops of unused yarn at the side of the work, weave them in neatly using the same method. Drop the current yarn A, bring the unused yarn B in front of A, then bring A in front of B and continue to work with A. The unused yarn B will be twisted into the side of the knitting and carried up the side without leaving long loops.

increasing stitches

Many of the projects in this book call for some shaping – otherwise all the items you ever knit would be square or rectangular. There are several ways to increase (explained below) and to decrease stitches (as shown on the following pages).

MAKE 1 (M1)

This increase is used when increasing stitches after a rib, such as on the Seed Stitch Beret (page 81). It is also used for shaping the thumb gusset on the gloves and mittens featured in this book. Use both the right- and left-twisting versions for a neat finish to the gusset. The new stitch is made between two existing stitches using the horizontal thread that lies between the stitches.

To twist M1 to the left

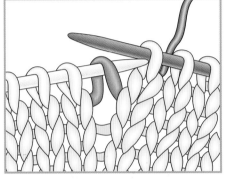

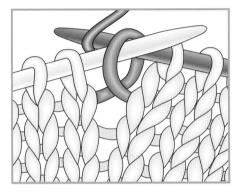

1 Knit to the point where the increase is to be made. Insert the tip of the left-hand needle under the running thread from front to back.

2 Knit this loop through the back to twist it. By twisting it you prevent a hole appearing where the made stitch is.

To twist M1 to the right

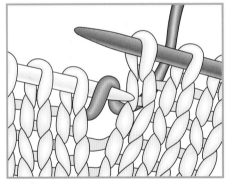

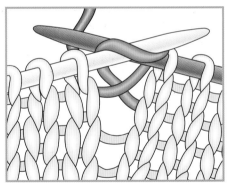

1 Knit to the point where the increase is to be made. Insert the tip of the left-hand needle under the running thread from back to front.

2 Knit this loop through the front to twist it.

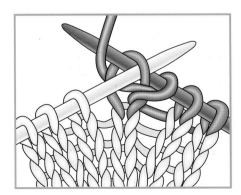

KNIT INTO FRONT AND BACK (KF&B)

This is an easy way to increase one stitch; you work into the front and back of the same stitch. Knit into the front of the stitch as usual. Do not slip the stitch off the left-hand needle, but knit into it again through the back of the loop. Then slip the original stitch off the left-hand needle.

KNIT INTO FRONT, BACK AND FRONT

This increases two stitches instead of one: simply knit into the front, back and then the front again of the same stitch.

(K1, P1, K1) ALL INTO SAME ST

This is also a way of increasing two stitches. Knit into the stitch as normal, do not slip the stitch off the left-hand needle but purl it as normal, and then knit into it again all into the front of the loop. This is used to make the bramble stitch on the Bramble Stitch Lacy Shawl (see pages 62–65).

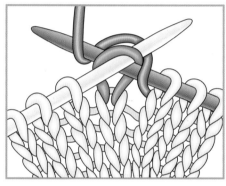

BETWEEN TWO KNIT STITCHES

You can increase one stitch between two knit stitches by (k1, yo, k1) or (k1, yfwd, k1). Bring the yarn forward between the two needles. Knit the next stitch, taking the yarn over the right needle.

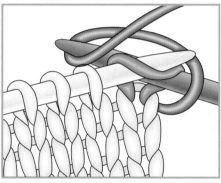

AT THE EDGE OF WORK

Sometimes you have to work a yarn over at the edge of the work, before the first stitch. The Bramble Stitch Lacy Shawl (pages 62–65) is shaped using this method; it adds a decorative lacy edge.

Before a knit stitch, bring the yarn forward as if to purl, knit the first stitch bringing the yarn over the right-hand needle as you do so.

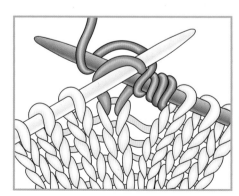

MULTIPLE YARN OVERS

These are used to make the holes on the edging for the Through the Keyhole Scarf (page 80).

Yo 4 times

Wrap the yarn around the needle four times. On the return row, you must knit into the first loop of the yarn over, purl into the second, knit into the third and purl into the fourth loop.

Yo 5 times

Wrap the yarn around the needle five times. On the return row, work into the first four loops of the yarn over as described for yo 4 times, and then knit into the fifth loop.

decreasing stitches

Decreases are used in many of the projects; they shape the tops of fingers in the gloves or the hat crowns to ensure a snug fit. These decreases are also used in the Making Waves Scarf (pages 54–57) to form the pattern.

DECREASING ONE STITCH

There are a number of ways to decrease one stitch.

K2tog

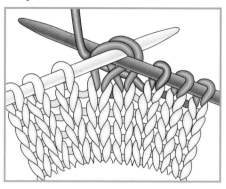

Knit to where the decrease is to be, insert the right-hand needle (as though to knit) through the next two stitches and knit them together as one stitch.

P2tog

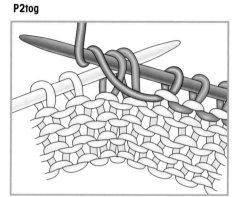

Purl to where the decrease is to be, insert the right-hand needle (as though to purl) through the next two stitches and purl them together as one stitch.

ssk or k2tog tbl

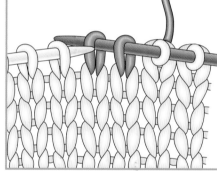

1 Slip two stitches knitwise one at a time from left-hand needle to right-hand needle (they will be twisted).

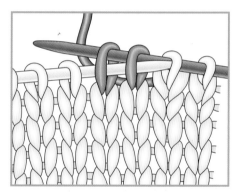

2 Insert the left-hand needle from left to right through the fronts of these two stitches and knit together as one stitch.

ssp or p2tog tbl

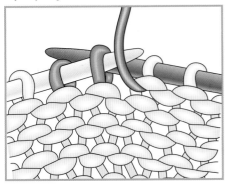

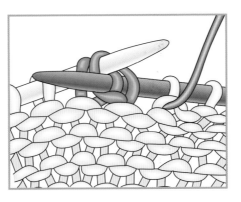

1 Slip two stitches knitwise, one at a time, from the left-hand needle to the right-hand needle (they will be twisted), pass these two stitches back to the left-hand needle in this twisted way.

2 Purl these two stitches together through the back loops.

DECREASING TWO STITCHES AT ONCE

There are various ways of decreasing two stitches at once.

K3tog

Work as k2tog, but knit three stitches together instead of two.

P3tog

Work as p2tog, but purl three stitches together instead of two.

K3tog tbl

Work as ssk (or k2tog tbl), but slip three stitches instead of two and knit them together.

P3tog tbl

Work as ssp, but slip three stitches instead of two and purl them together through the backs of the loops.

sl2tog-k1-psso

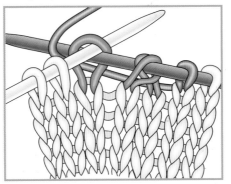

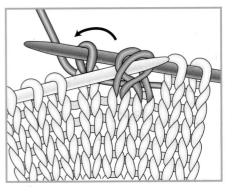

1 Insert the right-hand needle into the next two stitches as if to knit them together, and slip them off together on to the right-hand needle without knitting them. Knit the next stitch.

2 With the tip of the left-hand needle, lift the two slipped stitches together over the knitted stitch and off the needle.

cables

I've used cables on the wristwarmers (pages 66–69) and for the poncho and wrap (pages 96–101). Cables are simply a way of twisting two sets of stitches to form a rope or of carrying stitches across the fabric. Use a cable needle to hold the stitches or a double-pointed needle if you find a cable needle too short to hold. If you find working the stitches off the cable needle awkward, replace them on to the left-hand needle to work them.

C4F (CABLE FOUR FRONT)

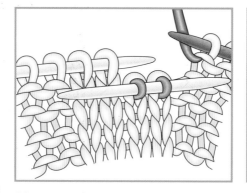

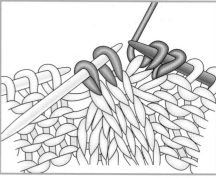

1 Slip the next two stitches from the left-hand needle on to a cable needle and hold at the front of the work.

2 Knit the next two stitches on the left-hand needle, then knit the two stitches from the cable needle.

C4B (CABLE FOUR BACK)

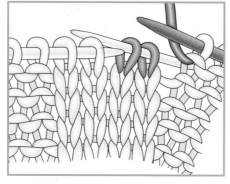

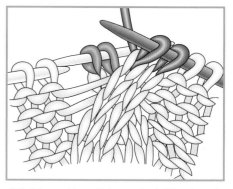

1 Slip the next two stitches from the left-hand needle on to a cable needle and hold at the back of the work.

2 Knit the next two stitches on the left-hand needle, then knit the two stitches from the cable needle.

KNIT PERFECT

Use a row counter or mark on paper each row worked to keep track of the rows between twists of the cable. To count the rows between twists of a cable, look for the row where you worked the twist; you will be able to identify this by following the path of the yarn from the last stitch of the cable to the first background stitch for a front-cross cable or from the last background stitch to the first stitch of the cable for a back-cross cable. On the row below this there will be no connecting strand of yarn between these same stitches. Count each strand for every row above the twist row.

C6F (CABLE SIX FRONT)

Work as C4F, but slip three stitches on to a cable needle instead of two and hold at front of work, and then knit three stitches.

C6B (CABLE SIX BACK)

Work as C4B, but slip three stitches on to a cable needle instead of two and hold at back of work, and then knit three stitches.

CR3L (CROSS THREE LEFT)

1 Slip the next two stitches from the left-hand needle on to a cable needle and hold at the front of the work.

2 Purl the next stitch on the left-hand needle, then knit the 2 stitches from the cable needle.

CR3R (CROSS THREE RIGHT)

1 Slip the next stitch from the left-hand needle on to a cable needle and hold at the back of the work.

2 Knit the next two stitches on the left-hand needle, then purl the stitch from the cable needle.

CR4L (CROSS FOUR LEFT)

Work as Cr3L, but slip three stitches on to a cable needle and hold at the front of the work, and then purl the next stitch. Knit the three stitches off the cable needle.

CR4R (CROSS FOUR RIGHT)

Work as Cr3R, but slip the next stitch onto a cable needle at back of work, then knit the next three stitches on the left-hand needle, before purling the stitch from the cable needle.

gloves and mittens

There are a number of gloves and mittens in this book. Many people can find these a slightly daunting prospect to knit – all those fingers to shape! But gloves are very satisfying to make, and simpler than they might seem, especially when made on two straight needles rather than the traditional method, which involves knitting in the round on double-pointed needles.

MITTENS

Mittens are very easy to knit and are a great introduction to knitting gloves.

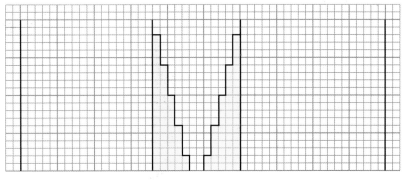

palm of mitten   *back of mitten*

Thumb gusset

The thumb on each hand is not added onto the side but more towards the palm. If you hold your hand out straight, palm up, you will see that your thumb naturally falls onto your palm rather than sticking out at the side. Stitches have to be added to accommodate the thumb; this is the thumb gusset. These stitches are made by working a M1 (see page 108) on each side of two stitches. Imagine the stitches on your needle divided into two; one half for the back of the mitten and the other half for the palm. The first increase is made before the first of the palm stitches and the second after two of the palm stitches.

Thumb

The thumb is worked on the stitches of the thumb gusset plus some extra stitches to fit around the back of the thumb, which need to be cast on using the cable cast-on method (see page 103). The thumb is shaped at the top to make a rounded end. The thumb seam is joined for the next bit of knitting. Because the two stitches at the beginning of the thumb gusset (between the increases) were used to knit the thumb, they need to be replaced to get back to the original number of stitches at the wrist. Two stitches are picked up across the cast-on edge of the thumb; one each side of the seam. The mitten is knitted straight to the top shaping; this is simple shaping to give the mitten a rounded finish.

Gloves

The rib, thumb gusset and thumb are worked exactly the same as those of a mitten (see above).

Fingers

Each finger is knitted using some of the stitches already on the needles and some extra stitches that are cast on. The second, third and fourth finger all pick up stitches from the base of the previous finger. The seam of the fourth finger is also the side seam, so no stitches are cast on here. The extra stitches are all picked up along the base of the third finger; four stitches instead of the usual two (see Love-heart Gloves, page 82).

KNIT PERFECT

On the thumb gusset, work a M1 twisted to the right as the first increase, and a M1 twisted to the left as the second one. You will see that the stitch twists away from the thumb gusset; it is a small detail, but I like to do it to add a finishing touch.

When you rejoin the yarn to pick up stitches at the base of the thumb or finger, leave a long end of yarn for sewing in. These joins are put under strain when you wear the gloves or mittens, so sew them securely. You can also use these ends to sew up any holes that might appear around the base of the fingers or thumb.

| 4th | 3rd | 2nd | 1st | 2nd | 3rd | 4th |

palm   back

original number of stitches

circular knitting

Circular knitting means that the knitted fabric is worked in rounds instead of rows; when you reach the end of a round you simply begin the next without turning the needles. You need a different needle from those you usually use for knitting; a circular needle is a length of flexible nylon wire fixed between two short needles and comes in several lengths. By knitting in rounds, you produce a tube of fabric with no seams. Shape the tube by increasing the number of stitches and you have a simple and quick way to make large garments such as ponchos.

WORKING WITH CIRCULAR NEEDLES

Cast on the required number of stitches on to one of the needle ends. Spread them evenly around the needle, making sure the cast-on edge faces inwards and is not twisted. The stitches should lie closely together and not be pulled too far apart. If the stitches are stretched when the needles are joined, you will need to use a shorter needle.

To identify the beginning of the round, place a marker in a contrast-colour yarn between the last and first cast-on stitch and slip this on every round. Bring the two needles together and knit the first stitch, pulling up the yarn to avoid a gap. Continue knitting each cast-on stitch to reach the marker. One round has been completed.

Begin the next round by slipping the marker.

CIRCULAR NEEDLES FOR FLAT KNITTING

Circular needles are also useful for knitting backwards and forwards for flat knitting. It is easier to work a large number of stitches, such as for the Beaded Beauties scarves (pages 74–77), on circular needles because all the stitches can easily be accommodated on the long needles and the weight of the fabric is held in front of you, on your lap, rather than at the end of long straight needles.

The Autumn Leaves Hooded Poncho (pages 44–47) is knitted on a circular needle. Two lengths are used; the longer one is substituted when stitches have been increased and become too many to be accommodated on the shorter length. The hood is knitted by using the circular needle for flat knitting (see below left).

fulling

Fulling is the process of washing woollen fabric to produce a felt-like fabric. This is often mistakenly called felting, but true felting is worked on carded unspun wool, whereas fulling is worked on a finished fabric. Fulling can only be worked on yarns that are 100% wool; it doesn't work on synthetics, cotton or wools that have been treated to be machine-washable. During fulling, the wool expands, fibres mesh together and individual stitches close up to form a soft fabric with a brushed appearance. The finished fabric will also shrink by up to 10% in length and width, although this varies with yarn and length of fulling. You should always knit an item intended for fulling bigger than you want it. Always do a test sample before fulling your knitted item; measure the sample so you can see how much it shrinks.

KNIT PERFECT

Always test samples of multi-coloured knitting to make sure all the yarns are colourfast.

Fulling only works on 100% wool; work a sample before you knit your project to make sure your yarn will full.

Brush the surface of the knitting when dry with a stiff brush; use a gently pulling or lifting action rather than a vigorous back and forwards motion.

HAND FULLING

Fulling depends on extremes of temperature, going from hot to cold, agitation by kneading and the use of soap; I use an olive oil soap. Do not use detergent or washing powder. Immerse the sample in hot (not boiling) water, using gloves to protect your hands. Rub the sample with the soap and start kneading the fabric without pulling, stretching or rubbing the knitting together. Remove the sample from the water frequently to check the fulling process. Rinse the soap out in cold water and pull the sample gently. If the stitches still move apart easily, continue the fulling. Keep up the temperature of the hot water. Stop when the fabric is dense and has a fuzzy appearance. Rinse the soap out and squeeze (do not wring) to remove excess water. Roll the sample up in a towel to soak up any remaining moisture and then lay it out flat, away from direct heat, to dry. Measure it and compare with the previous measurements; this will give you a guide as to how much your knitted item will shrink.

FULLING MITTENS

Put a coloured thread on the right-hand glove so you can identify right from left. Start the fulling process as described above. From time to time put the gloves on (while wearing washing-up gloves to protect your hands) and check the size. If the thumbs are not fulling as fast as the rest of the mitten, concentrate on them for a while, rubbing and pushing into shape. When the mittens have successfully fulled and are the right size, rinse, squeeze out the excess water and roll in a towel to soak up any remaining moisture. Lay out flat to dry, pulling any seams and edges straight.

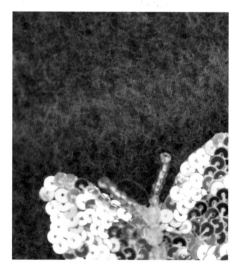

FULLING SCARVES

Full scarves before putting on fringes or embellishments; the fringe will full and turn into dreadlocks. Keep checking that the scarf is fulling at the same rate along its length; some parts may be narrower than others. When fulled, lay out flat to dry.

FULLING HATS

Keep measuring the hat during fulling around the circumference to make sure that it doesn't shrink too much. At some point, when the fulling is almost complete, rinse the hat out in cold water, squeeze out the excess water and try it on just to make sure. Complete the fulling. To dry it, you could place it over a small bowl; this will stop creases forming. Do not try to stretch it over something too big. Alternatively, lay out flat and keep turning during drying.

finishing techniques

When you have finished knitting all the pieces for your project, you should press them before making up. The knitted pieces will look flatter and you can pull out any side edges so that they are straight. Before pressing, sew in all yarn ends but don't trim them. During pressing, the knitting will stretch and yarn ends can pull through. Wait until the pieces have been pressed.

STEAM PRESSING

This is the method that I use most for natural yarns such as pure wool or those with a high wool content. Some yarns with a high synthetic fibre content, such as polyester and nylon, will not stand the high temperature needed for steaming so should never be steamed. Always check the ball band before steaming or test on your gauge square first.

Using rustproof pins, pin the knitted piece out, wrong side up, onto an ironing board. Do not pin out any ribs; they will lose their elasticity. Leave these unstretched. If the piece is too big, like the shawl or scarves, make a pressing board from a folded blanket covered with a sheet. Lay a clean cotton cloth over the pinned-out piece to protect it. Set the steam iron on an appropriate heat setting for the yarn. Hold the iron close to the surface of the knitting without touching it. Do not press the iron on to the knitted fabric. Let the steam penetrate the fabric. Remove the cloth and allow the fabric to dry before unpinning.

WET PRESSING

This is an alternative to steam pressing and is better for synthetics or fancy yarns. Pin out the pieces onto a pressing board, as above. Wet a clean cotton cloth and wring out the excess water until it is just damp. Place it over the pinned-out piece (avoiding any ribs) and leave to dry away from direct heat. When the cloth is completely dry, remove it. Make sure the knitted pieces are also dry before you take out the pins and remove them from the board.

SEWING UP

Whenever possible, sew the pieces together with the yarn they are knitted from. If the yarn is something that will break easily or is textured, like an eyelash yarn or bouclé, use a plain yarn in a matching colour. Do not use the long ends left after knitting the pieces to sew up with; if you do use them and you have to unpick the item for any reason, the ends may start to unravel the knitting. Use a tapestry needle and an 18in (45cm) length of yarn, so the yarn doesn't fray by being passed through the fabric too frequently.

Mattress stitch

To get an invisible seam, use mattress stitch. This is worked from the right side, making it easier to match stripes and shaping details, such as on the top of a hat. Secure the sewing yarn by weaving it down the edge of one of the pieces, bringing it to the front on the first row between the corner and second stitches. Place the two pieces to be joined side by side on a flat surface.

Joining two pieces of stockinette stitch

Having secured the yarn, take the needle across to the opposite side and insert it into the first row between the first and second stitches from front to back. Take it under the horizontal strand of the row above and pull the yarn through. Take the needle across to the first edge, insert the needle into the first row between stitches, again from front to back, and take it under the horizontal strands of the two rows above. Pull the yarn through. Insert the needle into the opposite edge again, in the same hole that the yarn came out of, and take it under the horizontal strands of the two rows above. Continue zigzagging between the edges, working under two rows each time. Pull the yarn up every few stitches to draw the seam together – but not too tightly, as the seam should not pucker the fabric.

Joining two pieces of reverse stockinette stitch

Having secured the yarn, take the needle across to the opposite side and insert it from front to back under the horizontal strand of the row above and pull the yarn through. Take the needle across to the other edge and insert it from front to back under the top loop of the second stitch. Take the needle back to the other edge and work under the strand of the row above. Continue in this way, inserting the needle under the top loop of the second stitch on one edge and under the horizontal strand between the first and second stitches on the other edge. One side of the seam takes in one and a half stitches, and the other takes in one stitch, but this weaves the reverse stockinette stitch together so the seam is invisible.

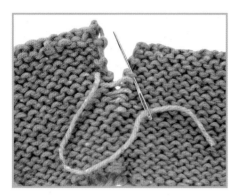

Joining ribs

In k1, p1 rib, work through the centre of the first stitch so that half a stitch is taken up on each side. Work under one row at a time. Pull the seam together and a whole stitch will be formed, so the rib is not interrupted by the seam. In k2, p2 rib, work as given for stockinette stitch, taking up a whole stitch to keep the rib correct.

Flat seam

Use this for joining on an edging, such as the one on the Through the Keyhole Scarf (page 80). Lay the edging on top of the main fabric, just covering the edge. Sew through both thicknesses, using a small running stitch. Do not pull the stitches too tightly or the fabrics will pucker.

PICKING UP STITCHES

One piece of knitting can be joined to another by picking up stitches and using these instead of casting them on. It eliminates a seam and makes a smoother, neater join. When knitting gloves, you have to pick up stitches for the next finger from the base of another one. The earflaps on the Shake Your Pompoms Ski Hat (pages 70–73) are also knitted from picked-up stitches, as is the hood on the Autumn Leaves Hooded Poncho (pages 44–47).

On a cast-on edge

Hold the work in your left hand with the right side facing. With a needle and the yarn in your right hand, insert the needle into the centre of the first cast-on stitch. Wrap the yarn knitwise around the needle and draw through a loop. Continue in this way, inserting the needle through the centre of each cast-on stitch until you have the correct number of stitches.

On stockinette stitch

The mitten flap of the Magic Mitten Gloves (pages 92–95) is picked up across the back of the gloves so you don't have to sew it on. Pick up the stitches as described above, but insert the needle under the top of the loop of each stitch.

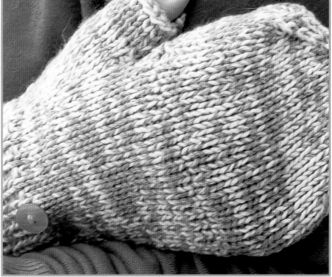

embroidery

Knitted accessories, particularly smaller items such as hats or gloves, can often be enhanced with a little embroidered detail, just to add a further touch of glamour. Some simple embroidery techniques are explained below.

KNIT PERFECT

Use embroidery threads, tapestry wools or knitting yarn; it should be the same or slightly thicker than the knitted yarn. Check that the threads are colourfast and will not shrink when washed. Work an embroidered sample and wash it if you are not certain.

Use a large-eyed blunt tapestry needle. Work the embroidery stitches loosely, don't pull too tightly or the knitted fabric will pucker. To begin the embroidery, weave the end of the thread through a few knitted stitches on the back of the fabric, working back through the thread to secure it; if you start with a knot, it may come undone during wear.

LAZY DAISY STITCH

This stitch is formed from individual chain stitches worked around a centre to create the petals of a flower. The loops are fastened with a small stitch. Bring the needle out at A. In one movement, push the needle down in the same place and bring it out at B, looping the thread under the needle tip. Take the needle back down at B, working over the loop, and bring it up at A for the next stitch.

CHAIN STITCH

Bring the needle out at A. In one movement, push the needle down in the same place and bring it out at B for the next stitch, looping the thread under the needle tip. To fill the chain stitch, work a straight stitch from the base to the top.

BUTTONHOLE STITCH

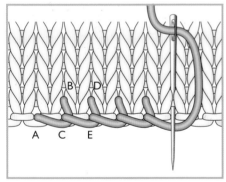

You can use this as a decorative edging along a knitted item, or to reinforce a button loop as on the Magic Mitten Gloves (pages 92–95). Often used to neaten raw edges, this stitch can be worked from left to right or from right to left. Bring the needle out at A. In one movement, take it down at B and back up at C, looping the thread under the needle tip. The next stitch is worked to the right, down at D and up at E. The horizontal threads should lie on the edge of the fabric.

SWISS DARNING

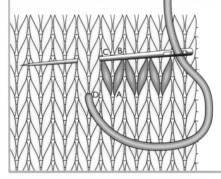

This stitch (also known as duplicate stitch) looks as though it has been knitted into the fabric; it follows the line of the yarn for the knit stitch on the right side of stockinette stitch. It is used to embroider small areas of colour such as a motif that would be tedious to knit, or you can use it to cover up any colours that you don't like in a stripe pattern, on the Striped Mittens for example (pages 38–39). Use the same thickness of yarn used for the knitting. Take care to insert the needle

between the strands and not to split the knitted stitches. The stitches will appear slightly raised on the surface of the knitting.

Horizontal stitches

Work from right to left, bringing the needle out at the base of the stitch (A). In one movement, take the thread around the top of the stitch by taking the needle down at B and up at C. In one movement, take the needle down at the base of the stitch (A) and up at the base of the next stitch (D). Continue across the row.

Vertical stitches

Work from bottom to top, bringing the needle out at the base of the stitch (A). Take the thread around the top of the stitch (B and C) and back down at the base (A). This time, bring the needle up at the base of the stitch above and continue up the line of knitted stitches.

knitting with beads

Beads are a lovely way to add some extra sparkle and texture to a really special knitted accessory. This simple technique is ideal for adding a large number of beads; you knit them in as you work, so you don't have to sew them all on later.

WORKING WITH BEADS

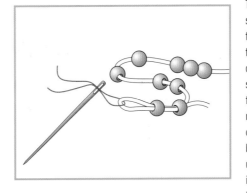

Thread the beads on to the ball of yarn before starting the knitting; the pattern instructions will tell you how many. To do this, choose a needle that will pass easily through the hole in the bead, and thread it with the two ends of a loop of sewing cotton. Thread the end of the yarn through the cotton loop. Now thread the beads on to the needle, pulling them down the sewing cotton and on to the yarn. Unwind sufficient yarn from the ball to accommodate the number of beads to be used and then rewind the ball to start knitting the item. Alternatively, if you are using a mix of beads, buttons and sequins with different sized holes, such as for the Beaded Beauties scarves (pages 74–77), dip the end of the yarn to be used for beading into PVA glue or clear nail varnish. Wait for it to dry and then trim the end into a point. Use the stiffened point as a needle to thread on the beads.

PB (place bead)

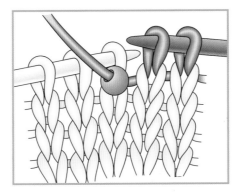

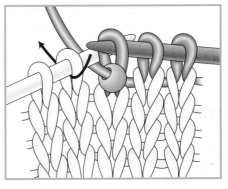

KNIT PERFECT

Beads should have a large enough hole to slide on to the yarn without being forced. If the fit is too tight, the yarn will wear and fray. The fabric should be knitted tightly enough so that the beads won't slip between the stitches to the wrong side. Always knit the stitches either side of the bead firmly.

1 On a right-side row, work to the position of the bead, knitting the last stitch worked firmly. Bring the yarn to the front of the work and push a bead down the yarn so that it rests next to the last stitch worked.

Sewing on sequins

The centre of the Classy Corsage (page 81) is filled with sequins topped with beads. Using a sewing cotton and a needle that will fit through the bead and sequin, secure the cotton to the knitted fabric. Thread on a sequin and then a bead. Take the needle back down through the hole on the sequin and through the knitted fabric. The bead will hold the sequin in place.

2 Slip the next stitch purlwise. Take the yarn back to the wrong side of the work and knit the next stitch firmly.

fringes and cords

You will often want to add some embellishment to a knitted accessory, such as adding a fringe to a scarf, or a cord or pompom to a hat. These effects are quite simple to achieve, but can be just the finishing touch you need to turn a knitted item into something really special.

FRINGE

Wrap yarn loosely around a piece of cardboard the required length of the fringe. Cut the wrapped strands at the bottom and remove the cardboard. Fold several lengths in half and, using a crochet or rug hook, pull the strands through the edge of the knitted piece from front to back by catching the fold with the hook. Pass the ends through the folded loop and pull to tighten the knot. Space each bunch of strands evenly along the edge. Trim the bottom of the fringe neatly to the finished length required.

TWISTED CORD

Strands of yarn twisted together will form a cord. The more strands you use, the thicker the cord will be. Cut lengths of yarn three times the finished length required and tie them together with a knot at each end. Hook one end over a doorknob or hook and, holding the other knotted end, stand back so that the strands are taut. Insert a pencil into the end and wind it to twist the strands. Keep the strands taut as you wind, twisting until the cord starts to fold up and twist around itself. Keeping the cord taut, remove the end from the doorknob and bring both knotted ends together. The cord will twist around itself. Ask someone to hold the middle or hang a weight from a hook on the middle of the cord to hold it taut as it twists. Small tassels can be made at either end by knotting the strands, cutting the looped end and then untying the knots from the other end. A textured cord is made by combining different yarns or colours.

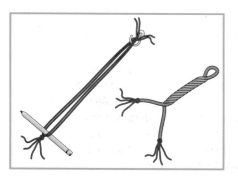

POMPOM

Cut two circles out of stiff cardboard. They should be the same diameter that you require for the finished pompom. Cut out a hole in the centre of each one half of this size. Cut a wedge shape out of the circles. Place them together and begin winding yarn around them until the hole in the centre is filled. Carefully cut through the loops all the way around, being careful not to let any yarn strands escape. Pull a length of yarn between the two pieces of cardboard, knot the two ends together and pull tightly around the centre of the pompom. Secure with a tight knot. Pull out the cardboard circles. Fluff up the pompom, trimming any uneven ends, but leave the two yarn ends for sewing onto your knitted item.

PLAITED CORD

This is an easy way to attach a plaited cord onto an edge, such as on the Shake Your Pompoms Ski Hat (see pages 70–73). Cut a number of strands of yarn three times the length of your finished plait. Thread them onto a large-eyed needle and use this to pull the strands through the edge where the plaited cord is to be. Pull them through halfway, evening up the ends. Divide the strands into three bunches. Make the plaited cord by passing the left-hand bunch over the centre bunch, and then the right-hand bunch over this new centre bunch. Repeat this until the cord is the right length. Tie a small knot into the end to prevent the plaited cord unravelling and trim the ends into a neat tassel.

TASSELS

Wrap the yarn loosely around a piece of card the required length of the tassel. Thread a long length of yarn under the strands at the top, fold in half and tie in tight knot, leaving two long ends. Cut the wrapped strands at the bottom and remove the cardboard. Thread one long end on to a tapestry needle, insert it through the top of the tassel and bring out 1in (2.5cm) below. Wrap the yarn several times around the tassel. Pass the needle through the middle of the wrapped strands to secure the long end, then insert the needle again up through the top of the tassel. Use the long ends to sew in place. Trim the bottom of the tassel neatly to make a straight edge.

knitted flowers

Knitted flowers can be used to add a beautifully feminine detail to an accessory. Use them alone as a corsage or a brooch, or add them to a hat for a flirty finish. Several ways of making flowers are detailed below.

DOUBLE FLOWER

With your chosen yarn, use needles two sizes smaller than those recommended on the ball band.

Make the outer ring by working 6 petals as given for Classy Corsage (page 81).

To make the inner ring of small petals (make 6):
Cast on 3 sts and knit 1 row.
Work rows 1 to 5 as given Classy Corsage. 9 sts.
Knit 5 rows.
Work from row 19 to the end.

Make up both rings of petals as given for Classy Corsage. Sew the inner ring of small petals into the outer ring. You could use a different colour or contrasting yarn for the centre petals. Fill the centre with beads, sequins or buttons, or add another layer of even smaller petals by working rows 1 to 3 (7 sts), knitting 5 rows and then working from row 23 to the end. Make a fuller single flower by working a ring of more than six petals.

FRINGED CORSAGE

This flower is fulled, so use a 100% wool yarn to make it.

Use your chosen yarn and needles the size recommended on the ball band. Cast on four times the number of stitches per 4in (10cm) as stated on the ball band. Work 4in (10cm) in st st. Bind off.
Full the knitting, following the instructions on page 115. Make sure the fabric is completely fulled because you will be cutting it.
Make even cuts about ½in (1cm) apart from one edge to within ¾in (1.5cm) of the opposite edge. Run a gathering thread through the base of the fabric and pull up into gathers. Form the flower by twisting it round and round from the centre. Work a few stitches through all layers to secure. Sew a button or a cluster of beads into the centre. Sew on a brooch pin.

For a shaded flower, you could work in stripes, using light to dark shades of one colour, or a combination of colours like dark purple and mauve, or dark red and pink.

ROSE

Small [Medium:Large] Petals (make 2 of each size)
With your chosen yarn and using needles two sizes smaller than those recommended on the ball band, cast on 3 [3:4] sts and purl 1 row.
Next Row (Kf&b – see page 108) 1 [2:2] times, k2 [1:2]. 4 [5:6] sts. P 1 row.
Next Row (Kf&b) twice, k2 [3:4]. 6 [7:8] sts.
Work 9 [11:13] rows in st st, starting with a p row.
Next Row (Ssk) twice, k2 [3:4]. 4 [5:6] sts.
P 1 row.
Next Row (Ssk) 1 [2:2] times, k2 [1:2].
P1 row.
Bind off, leave a long end for sewing up. Sew in other end of yarn.
Take a small petal, thread the long yarn end onto a large needle and use it to gather the straight edge with a running stitch. Curl the petal around itself with the st st side facing inwards and secure with a few stitches. Gather the second small petal in the same way, curl around the first petal and sew them together at the base. Continue to build up the rose with the two medium and two large petals, overlapping them. Sew on a brooch pin.

SPIKY FLOWER

With your chosen yarn and using needles two sizes smaller than those recommended on the ball band, cast on 5 sts.
Foundation Row K1, yo, k2 and turn.
Row 1 P4.
Row 2 K1, yo, k5.
Row 3 P7.
Row 4 K1, yo, k4 and turn.
Row 5 P6.
Row 6 K1, yo, k7.
Row 7 P9.
Row 8 K1, yo, k6 and turn.
Row 9 P8.
Row 10 K1, yo, k9.
Row 11 P11.
Row 12 Bind off 6 sts, k1 (last st used in binding off), yo, k2 and turn.
Rep these 12 rows 4 times more.
Work rows 1 to 7.
Row 8 Bind off 4 sts, k1, yo, k2 and turn.
Rep these 8 rows 4 times more.
Work rows 1 to 3.
Row 4 Bind off 2 sts, k1 (last st used in binding off), yo, k2.
Rep these 4 rows 3 times more then rows 1 to 3 again.
Bind off.
Run a gathering thread around the base of the flower. Pull up and arrange the three sets of petals into three layers. Work a few stitches through all layers to secure. Sew a button into the centre. Sew on a brooch pin.

troubleshooting

Even the most accomplished knitters make mistakes and come up against challenges, so don't be disheartened if you go wrong occasionally. These techniques show you the easy way to rectify your mistakes and find the way forward.

DROPPED STITCHES

A dropped stitch is a stitch that has fallen off your needle and has unravelled down a few rows, creating a ladder. The sooner you spot that you have dropped a stitch the easier it is to rectify the mistake. Get into the habit of checking your knitting every few rows.

Knit stitch dropped one row below

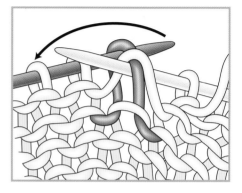

Insert the right needle through the front of the dropped stitch and then pick up the strand of yarn behind it. With the tip of the left needle, pass the stitch over the strand and off the needle.

Purl stitch dropped one row below

Insert the right needle through the back of the dropped stitch and then pick up the yarn strand in front of it. With the left needle, pass the stitch over the strand and off the needle.

Stitch dropped several rows below

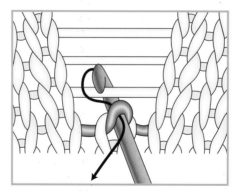

Find the dropped stitch – it will be a loop at the base of a ladder of strands of yarn. Insert a crochet hook through the front of the loop of the dropped stitch, catch the yarn strand immediately above it and pull through the stitch. Repeat for all the strands of the ladder until you reach the top. Slip the stitch back onto the left-hand needle.

To pick up a dropped purl stitch, work as given for a knit stitch but turn your work around so that you are working on the wrong side of the fabric. If more than one stitch has been dropped, slip the others on to a safety pin to stop them running any further, while you pick them up one by one. If you drop a stitch and do not notice it until a lot of knitting later, the ladder will have closed up at the top and there will be no strands of yarn to pick up with the crochet hook. Unfortunately, the only solution is to unravel your work back to the dropped stitch. If you try to pick it up by stealing yarn from the neighbouring stitches, it will create an area of tightened stitches and spoil your knitting.

UNRAVELLING ONE ROW

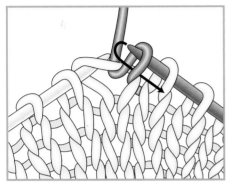

If you have made an error in the stitches that you have just worked on the right needle, for example in a stitch pattern or knitting when you should have purled, there is no need to take the work off the needle to unravel back to that point. You can just unravel, stitch by stitch, back to the error. Insert the left needle into the stitch below from the front, drop the stitch off the right needle and pull the yarn. Repeat this for each stitch back to the error. Work in the same way for purl stitches.

UNRAVELLING SEVERAL ROWS

If you have to unravel several rows, slip the needles out of the stitches carefully, gather the work up into one hand and unravel each row to the row above the error. Do not be tempted to lay the work out flat to do this, as you are more likely to pull the stitches roughly, which often results in you pulling out more than you want. Replace the stitches on to the needle and then unravel the last row carefully as given above. By doing this you have more control over the final row and are less likely to drop or miss any stitches. If you find that after unravelling, your needle is facing the wrong way, slip the stitches purlwise back onto another needle so that you are ready to knit. If you have a suitably sized double-pointed or circular needle, you can use this and then be able to work straight off either end of it.

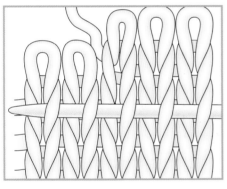

If you are using a slippery yarn or one that will not unravel easily, such as a hairy yarn, or if you are nervous about dropping stitches during unravelling, you can pick up stitches in the row below the error and then unravel knowing the stitches are safe on a needle. Take a spare needle that is smaller than that used for the knitting and weave it through the first loop and over the second loop of each stitch on the row below the mistake. Then pull the work back to these stitches. Make sure you put aside the smaller needle and pick up the correct size to continue knitting.

If you are working a cable or stitch pattern, you should pick the nearest row to the error without too much patterning and where you can see the stitches clearly.

RUNNING OUT OF YARN

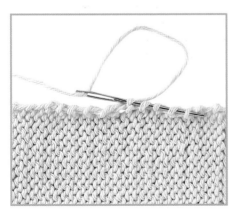

When you run out of yarn and need to start a new ball or need to change to another colour, always start it at the beginning of a row or at a seam edge where the ends can be woven in neatly.

Simply drop the old yarn, wrap the new yarn around the needle and work a few stitches. Tie the two ends securely together at the beginning of the row so neither one will work its way free and unravel your stitches. When you have finished the piece, undo the knot and weave one end up the edge for a couple of inches, and then double back

SPLIT YARN

You can easily split a strand of yarn if you are working fast, or, if you are using a yarn mix of several strands, it is easy to miss working through one of the strands. You should go back and rework it correctly, since any split like this will show up on your fabric. Use one of the unravelling methods described to go back to the split stitch.

INCOMPLETE STITCHES

These occur where you have wrapped the yarn around the needle but it has not been pulled through the old stitch to form a new stitch. The yarn strand will be on the needle next to the unworked stitch. Work the stitch properly with the yarn strand as given for dropped stitches.

CABLES

If you have twisted a cable the wrong way, and you have spotted it within a few rows, unravel the cable stitches only and reknit by using the long loops of yarn released by unravelling. If the error is a long way down the piece and the cable has been twisted again after the error, you will have to unravel the work and reknit all of it.

SNAGGED STITCHES

If you snag a stitch, a loop of yarn is pulled out, drawing up tightly several stitches around it. Using a tapestry needle, ease the extra yarn back through the distorted stitches, one by one, starting with the stitch closest to the snag and yarn loop.

over a few stitches to secure the end. Make sure you haven't pulled it too tightly and distorted the edge. Weave the other end down the edge using the same method.

If you are coming to the end of a ball, to see if you have enough yarn to work one more row, lay the knitting flat and measure the yarn four times across the width. This will be sufficient to work one row of stockinette stitch; textured and cabled fabric will need more yarn. When in doubt, join in a new ball of yarn to avoid running out of yarn halfway through and having to unravel stitches.

aftercare

Hand-knitted items need to be looked after with some love and care. After you've taken all the effort to make something beautiful, put a little time into keeping it looking good.

KNIT PERFECT

If in doubt, wash your gauge swatch gently and see how that reacts. If nothing serious happens, then you should be able to hand-wash your knitting carefully.

Hand-dyed yarns, dark colours and some denim yarns contain a lot of excess dye that will wash out. Wash these yarns separately.

Mohair and hairy yarns lose their fluffiness when washed, so use a soft brush to gently lift the fibres again. Use a gently pulling or lifting action rather than a vigorous back and forwards motion. Fancy fashion yarns can also lose some of their loftiness. For these, do not use a brush, but instead use the flat of your hand to rub across the surface of the knitting to restore the effect.

KNITTING NOTEBOOK

I always keep a ball band from each piece of knitting that I do pasted into a notebook. I also keep a small wrapping of the yarn, as a reminder and also for any mending that I might have to do in the future. The care instructions on the ball band are the best advice to follow when cleaning your knitted items. Instead of writing out long instructions, yarn companies use the same care symbols found on other garments. Look out for yarns that should be dry cleaned only.

WASHING

You can either hand- or machine-wash knitted items, according to the care instructions on the ball band. I would always recommend hand washing; there is more control over the process. It is often difficult to stop a machine in mid-cycle if something goes wrong.

Before washing, remove any non-washable trims. The sequin appliqué on the Full of Fun Mittens (pages 40–41) should be removed and if you use ceramic buttons as a trim, remove these too. Usually any trim or special button will have care instructions with it. The washing information below refers to both natural and synthetic fibres (that are suitable for hand-washing).

Use cool or lukewarm water and use the same temperature for washing and rinsing, avoiding the extremes of temperature that result in fulling (see page 115). Using a sink or large washing-up bowl, dissolve soap flakes or a special wool-washing solution in lukewarm water. If the soap flakes don't dissolve, add them to hot water, dissolve them and then add plenty of cold water for the right temperature. Lay the knitted item flat and squeeze the soap through the fibres; do not rub or twist the knitting. Take it out of the water, supporting its weight with both hands to stop it stretching. Squeeze out the excess soap and water; do not wring, you will distort the stitches.

RINSING

Refill the sink with clear water of the same temperature as that used for washing. Again, squeeze the water through the knitting; do not pull it out of the water as it is very heavy when waterlogged and will stretch. Rinse it several times, replacing the water each time, until the water runs clear of soap. Take it out of the water, supporting its weight and squeeze out the excess water.

DRYING

Roll the knitting in a colourfast towel to soak up the water. Lay it out flat on a dry towel, pull it back into shape and straighten edges, and leave to dry away from direct heat. If it has any creases or is out of shape when dry, steam press it (see page 116). If it is a large item, like the Classic Cabled Poncho (pages 96–99), or you are washing several items, you can use the spin cycle on your washing machine to remove excess water. Place the knitting in a pillowcase and tie the end closed. This will stop the knitting being stretched and the stitches catching on anything. Lay the knitting out flat to dry completely. Never use a tumble dryer.

MACHINE WASHING

Follow the washing instructions on the ball band carefully. You should use a delicates or cool-wash cycle with a short spin. Place the knitting in a pillowcase, tying the end closed. Remove the knitting as soon as the wash has ended, otherwise it will be badly creased. Lay out flat to dry.

STORING KNITTING

Store knitting neatly folded in clean, fabric bags to protect them from dust. Fabric bags allow the knitting to breathe; plastic bags tend to make natural fibres sweat and become damp. Add a moth-repellent, such as mothballs, to wool items. Air the knitting outside before wearing.

yarns used

Below are listed the specific yarns that were used for the projects in this book, should you wish to recreate them exactly as we have. Yarn companies frequently discontinue colours or yarns, and replace them with new yarns. Therefore, you may find that some of the yarns or colours below are no longer available. However, by referring to the yarn descriptions on the project pages, you will have no trouble finding a substitute.

SUBSTITUTING YARNS

To work out how much replacement yarn you need follow these simple steps. Use it for each colour or yarn used in the project.

1 The number of balls of the recommended yarn x the number of yards/metres per ball = A

2 The number of yards/metres per ball of the replacement yarn = B

3 A ÷ B = number of balls of replacement yarn.

Page 20 Gorgeous Garter Stitch
Over the Rainbow Stripey Scarf

2 x 3½oz (100g) balls of Noro Iro (75% wool/25% silk – 131yd/120m per ball) in colour 26

All Wrapped Up

9 x 1¾oz (50g) hanks of Louisa Harding Sari Ribbon (90% polyamide/10% metallic – 66yd/60m per hank) in colour 3

Simply Slinky Scarf

4 x 1¾oz (50g) hanks of Colinette Mercury (100% viscose – 68yd/62m per hank) in colour 146 Popsicle

Swatch

GGH Velour (100% nylon – 63yd/58m per ball) in colour 13

Page 28 Heads Up Hat

2 x 7/8oz (25g) balls of GGH Soft Kid (70% super kid mohair/25% nylon/5% wool – 150yd/138m per ball) in colour 13

Swatch with beads

South West Trading Company Oasis (100% soy silk™ – 240yd/220m per ball) in colour 502

Swatch with rose

Rowan Rowanspun 4ply (100% wool – 162yd/90m per ball) in colour 707

Page 32 Smitten Mittens
Simple Mittens

1 x 3½oz (100g) hank of Colinette Skye (100% wool – 150yd/138m per ball) in colour 89 dark umber

Embroidered Mittens

2 x 1¾oz (50g) balls of Debbie Bliss Alpaca Silk (80% alpaca/20% silk – 71yd/65m per ball) in colour 03 and oddments of DK wool for embroidery

Striped Mittens

Oddments of DK yarns in at least 10 colours

Full of Fun Mittens

2 x 1¾oz (50g) balls of Noro Kureyon (100% wool – 109yd/100m per ball) in colour 147

Funky Fur Mittens

A 1 x 1¾oz (50g) ball of Sirdar Boa (100% polyester – 102yd/93m per ball) in colour 24

B 1 x 1¾oz (50g) ball Artesano Alpaca (100% alpaca yarn – 131yd/120m per ball) in colour 57

Page 44 Autumn Leaves Hooded Poncho

5 x 3½oz (100g) hanks of Colinette Prism (wool with cotton twist – 130yd/120m per hank) in colour 145 frangipani

Swatch

Sirdar Funky Fur (100% polyester – 98yd/90m per ball) in colour 511, GGH Domino in colour 3 (44% cotton/43% acrylic/13% polyester – 136yd/125m per ball) and Twilleys Goldfingering (80% viscose/20% metallized polyester – 218yd/200m per 1¾oz/50g ball) in colour 05

Page 48 Good Things Come in Threes
Main Colourway
Whole Set

A 5 x 1¾oz (50g) balls of Rowan Scottish Tweed DK (100% wool – 123yd/113m per ball) in colour 005 Lavender

B 5 x 7/8oz (25g) balls of Rowan Lurex Shimmer (80% viscose/20% polyester 104yd/95m per ball) in colour 338 Bedazzled

C 2 x 7/8oz (25g) balls of Rowan Kidsilk Haze (70% super kid mohair/30% silk – 229yd/210m per ball) in colour 600 Dewberry

On the Fringes Scarf

3 x 1¾oz (50g) balls of yarn A (as above)

3 x 7/8oz (25g) balls of yarn B (as above)

2 x 7/8oz (25g) balls of yarn C (as above)

Flowered-up Hat

1 x 1¾oz (50g) balls of yarn A (as above)

2 x 7/8oz (25g) balls of yarn B (as above)

1 x 7/8oz (25g) balls of yarn C (as above)

Ribby Wristwarmers

1 x 1¾oz (50g) balls of yarn A (as above)

1 x 7/8oz (25g) balls of yarn B (as above)

1 x 7/8oz (25g) balls of yarn C (as above)

Swatch

A Debbie Bliss Baby Cashmerino (55% merino wool/33% microfibre/12% cashmere – 136yd125m per 1¾oz/50g ball) in colour 614

B GGH Velour (100% nylon – 63yd/58m per 7/8oz/25g ball) in colour 10

C Rowan Kidsilk Haze (70% super kid mohair/30% silk – 229yd/210m per 7/8oz/25g ball) in colour 597

Page 54 Making Waves Scarf

A 1 x 1¾oz (50g) balls of Jaeger Matchmaker DK (100% wool – 131yd/120m per ball) in colour 899

B 1 x 1¾oz (50g) balls of Louisa Harding Impression (84% nylon/16% mohair – 154yd/140m per ball) in colour 02

Swatch

Rowan Scottish Tweed DK (100% wool – 123yd/
113m per ball) in colour 016 and GGH Safari
(78% linen/22% nylon – 152yd/140m per ball) in
colour 101

Page 58 Smart Girl Gloves

A 1 x 1¾oz (50g) ball of Jaeger Luxury Tweed
(65% wool/35% alpaca – 197yd/180m per ball) in
colour 820

B 1 x 1¾oz (50g) ball of Jo Sharp 8ply DK (100%
wool – 107yd/98m per ball) in colour 005 camel

Page 62 Bramble Stitch Lacy Shawl

4 x ⅞oz (25g) balls of GGH Soft-Kid (70% super
kid mohair/25% nylon/5% wool – 150yd/138m
per ball) in colour 32

Summer Swatch

Rowan 4ply Cotton (100% cotton – 186yd/170m
per ball) in colour 126

Winter Swatch

Noro Kureyon (100% wool – 109yd/100m) in
colour 154

Page 66 In a Twist Wristwarmers

2 x 1¾oz (50g) balls of Debbie Bliss Cashmerino
Aran (55% wool/33% microfibre/12% cashmere
– 98yd/90m per ball) in colour 607

Swatch

Debbie Bliss Maya (100% wool – 137yd/126m per
3½oz/100g ball) in colour 07

Page 70 Shake Your Pompoms Ski Hat

A 1 x 3½oz (100g) ball of Rowan Scottish Tweed
Aran (100% wool – 186yd/170m per ball) in
colour 10 brill pink

B 1 x ⅞oz (25g) ball of Rowan Lurex Shimmer
(80% viscose/20% polyester – 104yd/95m per
ball) in colour 336

Cream swatch

Jaeger Shetland Tweed Aran (80% wool/20%
alpaca – 182yd/166m per ball) in colour 04
and Rowan Kid Classic (70% lambswool/26%
kid mohair/4% nylon – 153yd/140m per ball) in
colour 828

Lilac swatch

Jaeger Matchmaker DK (100% wool – 131yd/
120m per ball) in colour 883 with Rowan Chunky
Cotton Chenille (100% cotton – 153yd/140m per
ball) in colour 389 and Rowan Rowanspun 4ply
(100% wool – 162yd/90m per ball) in colour 725

Page 74 Beaded Beauties
Summer Scorcher Scarf

1 x 1¾oz (50g) balls of GGH Safari (78%
linen/22% nylon – 152yd/140m per ball) in each
of colours 5 (pink) and 6 (mauve)

1 x ⅞oz (25g) balls of GGH Velour (100% nylon
– 63yd/58m per ball) in colour 1 (cream)

1 x 1¾oz (50g) ball of GGH Domino (44%
cotton/43% acrylic/13% polyester – 136yd/125m
per ball) in colour 18 (cream)

1 x 1¾oz (50g) balls of GGH Mystik (54%
cotton/46% viscose – 119yd/110m per ball) in
colour 93 (mauve)

Winter Warmer Scarf

1 x 1¾oz (50g) balls of Jaeger Matchmaker DK
(100% wool – 131yd/120m per ball) in each of
colours 791 (brown) and 898 (pumpkin)

1 x 1¾oz (50g) balls of Jaeger Trinity (40%
silk/35% cotton/25% polyamide fibre – 218yd/
200m per ball) in colour 452 (tan)

1 x 1¾oz (50g) balls of Rowan Scottish Tweed
(100% wool – 123yd/113m per ball) in colour 17 (red)

1 x ⅞oz (25g) balls of Louisa Harding Kimono
Angora (70% angora/25% wool/5% nylon
– 124yd/112m per ball) in colour 1 (gold/pink)

Page 78 Cashmere Chic Set
Whole Set

7 x 1¾oz (50g) balls of Rowan Classic Yarns
Cashsoft DK (57% wool/33% microfibre/10%
cashmere – 142yd/130m per ball) in colour 521

Through the Keyhole Scarf

3 x 1¾oz (50g) balls of above yarn

Seed Stitch Beret

2 x 1¾oz (50g) balls of above yarn

Classy Corsage

1 x 1¾oz (50g) balls of above yarn

Love-Heart Gloves

2 x 1¾oz (50g) balls of above yarn

Page 84 Mighty Mitred Squares

6 x 1¾oz (50g) balls of Noro Kureyon (100% wool
– 109yd/100m per ball) in colour 139

Swatch

Noro Kureyon (100% wool – 109yd/100m per ball)
in colour 147

Page 88 Weekender Cap

3 x 1¾oz (50g) balls of Debbie Bliss cotton denim
aran (100% cotton – 74yd/68m per ball) in colour 02

Urban swatch

Sirdar Snuggly Tiny Tots DK (90% acrylic/10%
polyester – 150yd/137m per ball) in colour 960
Rowan Lurex Shimmer (80% viscose/20%

polyester –104yd/95m per ball) in colour 330

Tweed swatch

Rowan Yorkshire Tweed 4ply (100% wool
– 120yd/110m per ball) in colour 270 with Jaeger
Matchmaker DK (100% wool – 131yd/120m per
ball) in colour 856, Jaeger Baby Merino DK (100%
merino wool – 131yd/120m per ball) in colour
194, Jamieson & Smith 2ply wool (100% Shetland
wool – 129yd/118m per ball) in colour 20

Page 92 Magic Mitten Gloves
Falling For You Gloves

1 x 1¾oz (50g) balls of Jaeger Matchmaker DK
(100% wool – 131yd/120m per ball) in each of
colours 898 (A), 899 (B), 877 (C), 862 (D) and
746 (E)

Soft 'n' subtle

1 x 1¾oz (50g) ball of Rowan Yarn Collection
Cashcotton 4ply (35% cotton/25% polyamide/18%
angora/13% viscose/9% cashmere – 197yd/180m
per ball) in each of colours 902 and 903

Page 96 Crossover Cables
Classic Cabled Poncho

11 x 3½oz (100g) hanks of Colinette Skye (100%
wool – 151yd/138m per hank) in colour 75 moss

Cobweb Cabled Wrap

9 x ⅞oz (25g) balls of Rowan Kidsilk Spray
(70% kid mohair/30% silk – 229yd/210m per ball)
in colour 574

Page 121 Flowers
Double Flower

Jaeger Trinity (40% silk/35% cotton/25%
polyamide fibre – 218yd/200m per 1ball) in colour
431

Rowan Wool Cotton (50% wool/50% cotton
– 122yd/113m per ball) in colour 943

Fringed Corsage

Noro Kureyon (100% wool – 109yd/100m per ball)
in colour 15

Rowan Yorkshire Tweed DK (100% wool – 123yd/
113m per ball) in colour 342

Rose

DMC Tapestry Wool in colours 7157, 7153 and
7151

Spiky Flower

DMC Tapestry Wool in colours 7372, 7016, 7014
and 7264

Rowan Denim (100% cotton – 101yd/93m per ball
in colour 229

suppliers

Contact the manufacturers for your local stockist or go to their websites for stockist and mail order information.

Artesano
(UK) Artesano Ltd, 28 Mansfield Road,
Reading, Berkshire, RG1 6AJ, UK
tel: +44 (0) 118 9503350
www.artesano.co.uk

Colinette
(USA) Unique Kolours
28 North Bacton Hill Road, Malvern, PA 19355, USA
tel: (800) 252 3934
www.uniquekolours.com
(UK) Colinette Yarns Ltd, Banwy Workshops, Llanfair
Caereinion, Powys, Wales, SY21 0SG
tel: 01938 810128
e-mail: feedback@colinette.com
www.colinette.co.uk

Debbie Bliss
www.debbieblissonline.com
(USA) Knitting Fever Inc.
315 Bayview Avenue, Amityville,
NY 11701, USA
tel: 001 516 5463600
e-mail: knittingfever@knittingfever.com
www.knittingfever.com
(UK) Designer Yarns Ltd,
Units 8–10 Newbridge Industrial Estate, Pitt Street,
Keighley, West Yorkshire, BD21 4PQ
tel: 01535 664222
www.designeryarns.uk.com
(AUS) Prestige Yarns Pty Ltd
P O Box 39, Bulli NSW 2516
AUSTRALIA
tel: +61 (0)2 4285 6669
e-mail: info@prestigeyarns.com
www.prestigeyarns.com

DMC
(USA) The DMC Corporation,
10 Port Kearney, South Kearney, NJ, 070732
tel: 973 589 0606
www.dmc-usa.com
(UK) DMC Creative World Ltd
Pullman Road, Wigston, Leicester, LE18 2DY.
tel: 0116 281 1040
www.dmc.com
(AUS) For a list of stockists go to their website at
www.dmc.com

GGH
www.ggh-garn.de
(USA) Muench Yarns Inc
1323 Scott Street, Petaluma, CA 94954-1135, USA
tel: (800) 733-9276
www.muenchyarns.com
e-mail: info@muenchyarns.com
(UK) Get Knitted
Unit 2B, Barton Hill Trading Estate, Herapath Street,
Barton Hill, Bristol BS5 9RD Tel: 0117 941 2600
www.getknitted.com
e-mail: sales@getknitted.com

Jaeger
(USA) Westminster Fibres Inc,
4 Townsend West, Suite 8, Nashua, NH 03063
tel: (603) 886 5041
e-mail: jaeger@westminsterfibers.com
(UK) Jaeger Handknits
Green Lane Mill, Holmfirth, HD9 2DX
tel: 01484 680050
e-mail: mail@knitrowan.com
(AUS) Australian Country Spinners
314-320 Albert Street, Brunswick, Victoria 3056
tel: 3 9380 3888
e-mail: sales@auspinners.com.au

Jo Sharp
www.josharp.com.au
(USA) JCA Inc.
35 Scales Lane, Townsend, MA 01469-1094
tel: (978) 597 8794
(UK) Get Knitted
Unit 2B, Barton Hill Trading Estate,
Herapath Street, Barton Hill, Bristol BS5 9RD
tel: 0117 941 2600
www.getknitted.com
e-mail: sales@getknitted.com
(AUS) Jo Sharp Pty Ltd, PO Box 1018, Fremantle,
Western Australia 6330
tel: +61 8 9430 9699
e-mail: yarn@josharp.com.au

Louisa Harding
www.louisaharding.co.uk
(USA) Knitting Fever Inc.
315 Bayview Avenue, Amityville, NY 11701, USA
tel: 001 516 5463600
e-mail: knittingfever@knittingfever.com
www.knittingfever.com
(UK) Get Knitted
Unit 2B, Barton Hill Trading Estate, Herapath Street,
Barton Hill, Bristol BS5 9RD
tel: 0117 941 2600
www.getknitted.com
e-mail: sales@getknitted.com

Noro
(USA) Knitting Fever Inc.
315 Bayview Avenue, Amityville, NY 11701, USA
tel: 001 516 5463600
e-mail: knittingfever@knittingfever.com
www.knittingfever.com
(UK) Designer Yarns Ltd,
Units 8-10 Newbridge Industrial Estate,
Pitt Street, Keighley, West Yorkshire, BD21 4PQ
tel: 01535 664222
www.designeryarns.uk.com
(AUS) Prestige Yarns Pty Ltd
P.O.Box 39, Bulli NSW 2516
tel: +61 02 4285 6669
www.prestigeyarns.com
e-mail: info@prestigeyarns.com

Rowan
www.knitrowan.com
(USA) Rowan USA,
4 Townsend West, Suite 8, Nashua, NH 03063
tel: (603) 886 5041
e-mail: rowan@westminsterfibers.com
(UK) Rowan, Green Lane Mill, Holmfirth, HD9 2DX
tel: 01484 681881
e-mail: mail@knitrowan.com
(AUS) Australian Country Spinners
314-320 Albert Street, Brunswick, Victoria 3056
tel: 3 9380 3888
e-mail: sales@auspinners.com.au

Rowan Classic Yarns
www.ryclassic.com
(USA) Westminster Fibres Inc,
4 Townsend West, Suite 8, Nashua, NH 03063
tel: (603) 886 5041
e-mail: ryc@westminsterfibers.com
(UK) RYC
Green Lane Mill, Holmfirth, HD9 2BR
tel: 01484 681881
e-mail: mail@ryclassic.com
(AUS) Australian Country Spinners
314-320 Albert Street, Brunswick, Victoria 3056
tel: 3 9380 3888
e-mail: sales@auspinners.com.au

Sirdar
www.sirdar.co.uk
(USA) Knitting Fever Inc.
315 Bayview Avenue, Amityville, NY 11701, USA
tel: 001 516 5463600
e-mail: knittingfever@knittingfever.com
www.knittingfever.com
(UK) Sirdar Spinning Ltd,
Flanshaw Lane, Alverthorpe, Wakefield, WF2 9ND
tel: 01924 371501
e-mail: enquiries@sirdar.co.uk
(AUS) Creative Images
PO Box 106, Hastings, Victoria 3915, Australia
tel: 03 5979 1555
e-mail: creative@peninsula.starway.net.au

South West Trading Company
(USA and AUS) For list of stockists go to their website
at www.soysilk.com
(UK) Get Knitted
Unit 2B, Barton Hill Trading Estate, Herapath Street,
Barton Hill, Bristol BS5 9RD
tel: 0117 941 2600
www.getknitted.com
e-mail: sales@getknitted.com

Twilleys
www.twilleys.co.uk
(UK) Twilleys of Stamford
Roman Mill, Stamford PE9 1BG
tel: 01780 752661
e-mail: twilleys@tbramsden.co.uk

index

acknowledgments

I would like to thank Sue Morgan at Viridian (getknitted.com) for supplying all the GGH and Jo Sharp yarns used in this book; DMC Creative World Ltd for the tapestry wools; and Sirdar for their yarns. Thanks also to Lorna Yabsley for the fantastic photography and the models for wearing the accessories so beautifully. At David & Charles, thanks go to Cheryl Brown, Jennifer Proverbs and Prudence Rogers for creating this book. Finally, thanks to Nicola Hodgson for editing and making sense of my manuscript.